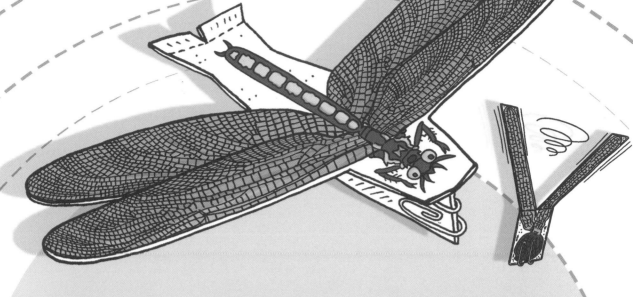

FLIGHT SCHOOL

Buster Books

WRITTEN, DRAWN AND CREATED BY
MIKE BARFIELD

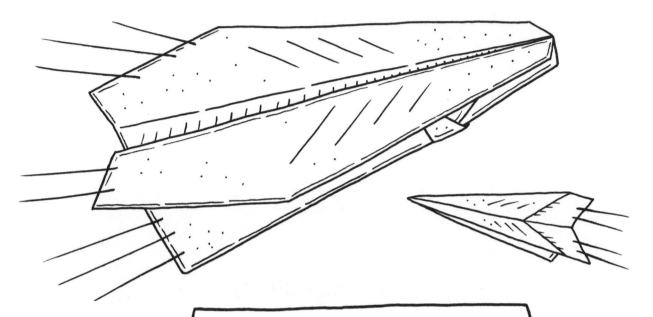

EDITED BY KATY LENNON
DESIGNED BY ZOE BRADLEY
COVER DESIGN BY ANGIE ALLISON
WITH SPECIAL THANKS TO FRANCES EVANS

This book was entirely written and drawn in North Yorkshire, England and is dedicated to the memory of that county's great aviation pioneer, Sir George Cayley.

First published in Great Britain in 2019 by Buster Books, an imprint of
Michael O'Mara Books Limited, 9 Lion Yard, Tremadoc Road, London SW4 7NQ

 www.mombooks.com/buster   BusterBooks   @Busterbooks

A CIP catalogue record for this book is available from the British Library.

ISBN: 978-1-78055-585-0

1 3 5 7 9 10 8 6 4 2

This book was printed in February 2019 by Leo Paper Products Ltd, Heshan Astros Printing Limited, Xuantan Temple Industrial Zone, Gulao Town, Heshan City, Guangdong Province, China

CONTENTS

ABOUT THE AUTHOR

Mike Barfield is a writer, cartoonist, poet and performer. He has worked in TV and radio, as well as in schools, libraries, museums and bookshops. He is the creator behind the *Destroy This Book* series.

INTRODUCTION

Welcome to Flight School. Get ready to learn lots of fantastic facts about the history of flight as you embark on a journey from a time before dinosaurs to the golden age of flight and beyond.

Along the way you'll get to make a fleet of fabulous flying models, including birds, beasts, plants, planes and even a jet-propelled space shuttle.

You will only need a few other items to get your models ready for take-off:

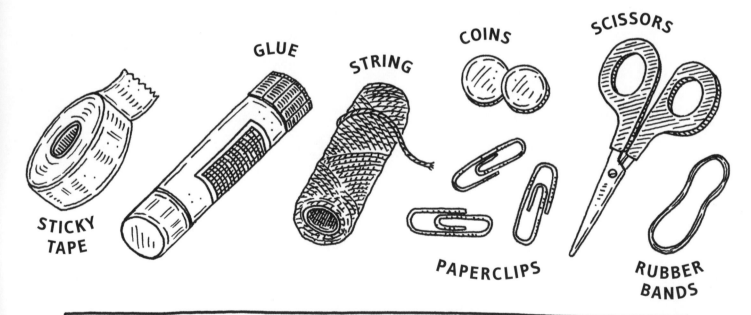

STICKY TAPE

GLUE

STRING

COINS

PAPERCLIPS

SCISSORS

RUBBER BANDS

All of the instructions you need are given on the model sheets in the second half of the book. Follow them all carefully and turn your home into an aerodrome!

HINTS AND TIPS

- Read all of the instructions on both sides of the model sheets before cutting anything out
- Be careful not to cut through the instructions
- If your models don't fly very far, make a few adjustments, like the ones suggested on page 5, and try again.

HOW THINGS FLY

Air makes flight possible on our planet. The action of a wing or rotor through the air can produce an upwards push or force that acts against gravity and keeps a flying animal or machine from falling to the ground.

A JET PLANE'S WING

HELICOPTER ROTORS

Four forces act on an object during flight:

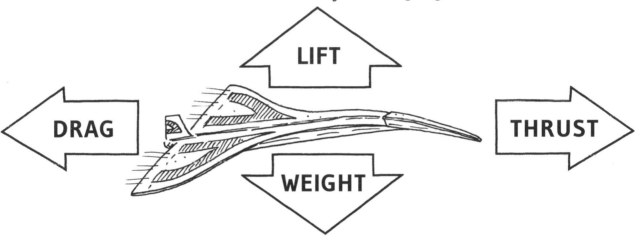

LIFT

DRAG

THRUST

WEIGHT

The upward force is called 'lift'. 'Weight' is the downward force due to gravity (the force that pulls objects towards the centre of the Earth). 'Thrust' propels a thing forwards and 'drag' slows it down. All of these forces need to be properly balanced for something to fly.

For aeroplanes, thrust is created by the engine, but for the models in this book it comes from your muscles. Flying animals use their muscles to provide both thrust and lift.

Technically, because these models don't have engines, they glide rather than fly. Gliding is a controlled form of falling to the ground.

ADJUSTMENTS

To make them fly well, some models need paperclips adding to them so that they are heavier at the front, or 'nose'. Curling the wing tips up or down can also help — this deflects air and helps the models rise or fall.

5

GIANT OF THE SWAMPS

Insects were the first animals to take to the air. Experts have found evidence in fossils that suggests insects developed wings around 360–300 million years ago in a period of time called the 'Carboniferous Period'. Having wings enabled insects to find new habitats, more food and other insects to mate with.

Some of these insects were flying giants.

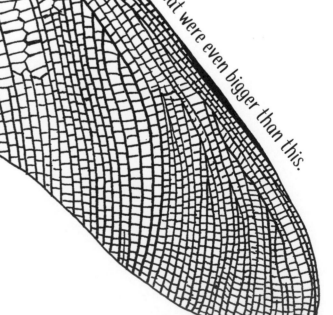

Meganeura could have had wings that were even bigger than this.

THE MODERN DRAGONFLY HAS A 12 CM WINGSPAN.

MEGANEURA HAD A 60–75 CM WINGSPAN.

Meganeura is one of the largest flying insects known to science. It hunted smaller insects and amphibians in swamps and forests, 300 million years ago.

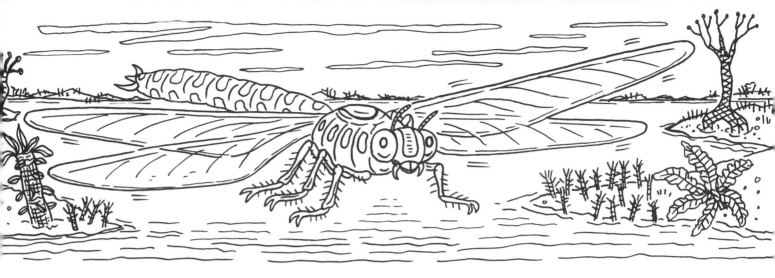

It is thought that *Meganeura* was able to grow so big because the air in the Carboniferous Period had more oxygen in it than our air does today. This meant that insects could be larger and still breathe efficiently.

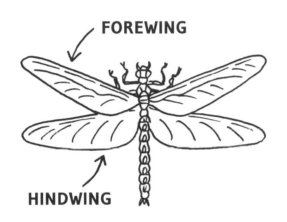

FOREWING

HINDWING

Dragonflies are very agile fliers. They can move each wing independently, allowing them to hover, glide and fly in all directions — including backwards.

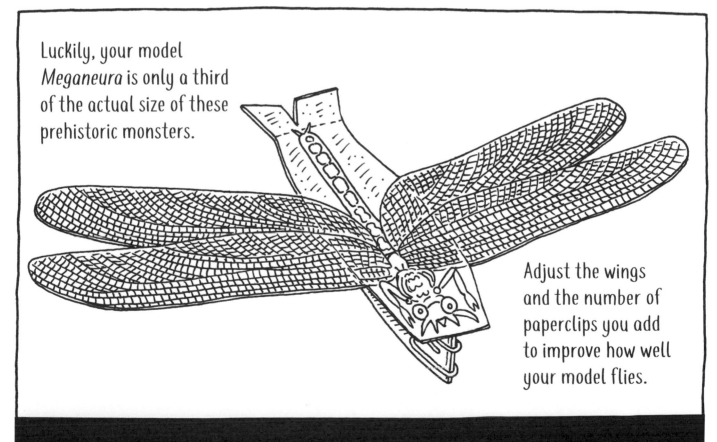

Luckily, your model *Meganeura* is only a third of the actual size of these prehistoric monsters.

Adjust the wings and the number of paperclips you add to improve how well your model flies.

MAKE A MODEL *MEGANEURA* ON PAGE 41.

INCREDIBLE INSECTS

Scientists say that insects account for roughly 90% of the animals on our planet. They estimate that there are 6–10 million species and at least 99% of them can fly.

The white witch moth of Central and South America has the largest wingspan of any living insect — up to 30 cm.

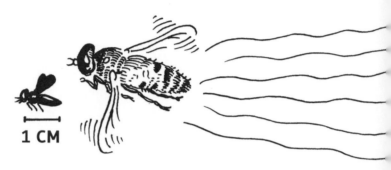

1 CM

Most insects have two pairs of wings, but houseflies have only one. Despite this, they can fly forwards, backwards, sideways and upside-down, making them very hard to swat.

The fastest flying insect is thought to be the horsefly. It is less than 1 cm long but scientists estimate that it can reach speeds of up to 145 kph.

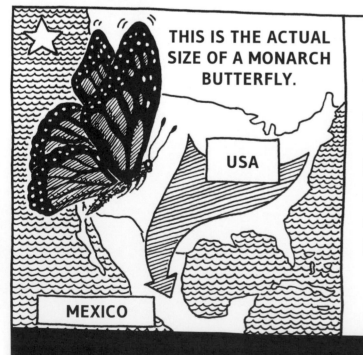

THIS IS THE ACTUAL SIZE OF A MONARCH BUTTERFLY.

USA

MEXICO

The monarch butterfly is an orange and black butterfly that migrates thousands of kilometres each year between the USA and Mexico. Weighing less than a paperclip, the monarch saves energy by flying slowly and gliding for long distances when possible.

MAKE A MODEL MONARCH BUTTERFLY ON PAGE 43.

FLYING FOSSILS

Fossil records reveal that the first flying vertebrates (animals with backbones) flew over Earth about 228 million years ago. Scientists called them pterosaurs, meaning 'winged lizards'. Their wings were made of skin, which stretched out between their legs and their extended claws.

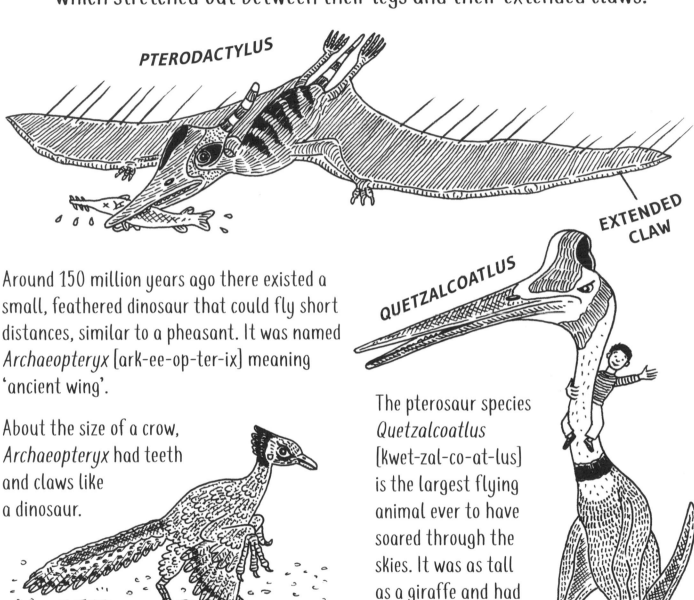

PTERODACTYLUS

QUETZALCOATLUS

EXTENDED CLAW

Around 150 million years ago there existed a small, feathered dinosaur that could fly short distances, similar to a pheasant. It was named *Archaeopteryx* [ark-ee-op-ter-ix] meaning 'ancient wing'.

About the size of a crow, *Archaeopteryx* had teeth and claws like a dinosaur.

ARCHAEOPTERYX

The pterosaur species *Quetzalcoatlus* [kwet-zal-co-at-lus] is the largest flying animal ever to have soared through the skies. It was as tall as a giraffe and had a 10 m wingspan.

The pterosaurs died out along with the dinosaurs approximately 66 million years ago. *Archaeopteryx* is also extinct, but its descendants live on today in the form of birds.

MAKE *ARCHAEOPTERYX* FLY AGAIN ON PAGE 45.

WINGED WONDERS

Birds are brilliant fliers. Descended from dinosaurs, their bodies are amazingly adapted for aviation. They have hollow bones so that they're not too heavy, big wing muscles and strong, but light, flexible feathers.

Birds' wings have a curved shape known as an airfoil. The top of the wing is curved, which means that the air pressure on top is less than below – this generates lift, allowing the bird to soar and glide.

HOW AIR FLOWS OVER THE WINGS

The keel bone is large and strong to provide a base for the wing muscles.

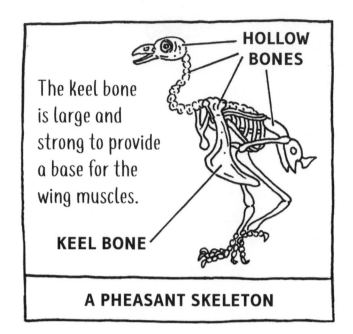

HOLLOW BONES

KEEL BONE

A PHEASANT SKELETON

The wings and body shapes of birds vary widely.
Different wing shapes have different functions. Here are a few of them:

ELLIPTICAL WINGS

- Types of birds: finches, song birds, kingfishers
- Useful for: short bursts of speed, agility

HIGH-SPEED WINGS

- Types of birds: swifts, swallows, hawks, falcons
- Useful for: 'sustained' (continued for a long time) fast flight, pursuit

HIGH-ASPECT RATIO WINGS

- Types of birds: albatrosses and other sea birds
- Useful for: sustained flight without flapping

SOARING WINGS

- Types of birds: condors, eagles, vultures
- Useful for: soaring on hot air, quick, easy movement

PEREGRINE FALCON

The peregrine falcon is the fastest bird on the planet. It can reach speeds of over 390 kph in a stooping dive — faster than a high-speed train or Formula 1 racing car.

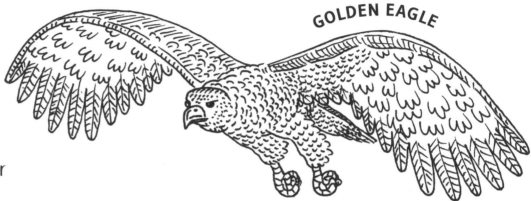

GOLDEN EAGLE

The golden eagle is the second fastest and can dive at up to 320 kph. It can also soar for long periods on updrafts of warm air known as 'thermals'.

The bird with the widest wingspan is the wandering albatross, which is found across the Southern Ocean. It can lock its wings into position and fly thousands of kilometres without landing.

WANDERING ALBATROSS

3.5 M WINGSPAN

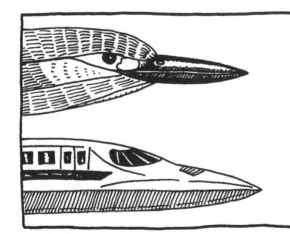

The kingfisher is a small, fast bird that dives into water to catch fish. It has a long, pointed beak that hardly makes a splash. This stream-lined shape was copied for the nose of the super-fast Japanese Shinkansen 'bullet' train, to make it move smoothly through the air.

MAKE A GOLDEN EAGLE ON PAGE 47.
MAKE A SPEEDING KINGFISHER ON PAGE 49.

FALLING WITH STYLE

Although many vertebrates are described as being able to fly, this is actually not always the case. Often they can only glide and are unable to fly properly. Bats are the only mammals capable of true sustained flight.

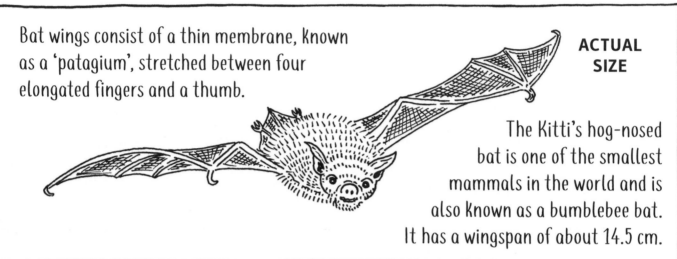

Bat wings consist of a thin membrane, known as a 'patagium', stretched between four elongated fingers and a thumb.

ACTUAL SIZE

The Kitti's hog-nosed bat is one of the smallest mammals in the world and is also known as a bumblebee bat. It has a wingspan of about 14.5 cm.

There are over 1,000 species of bats. Most are nocturnal and eat either fruit or insects. Their super-thin wings make them quick and nimble fliers.

The Brazilian free-tailed bat has been clocked at a super-fast 160 kph in horizontal flight — a world record speed for any animal.

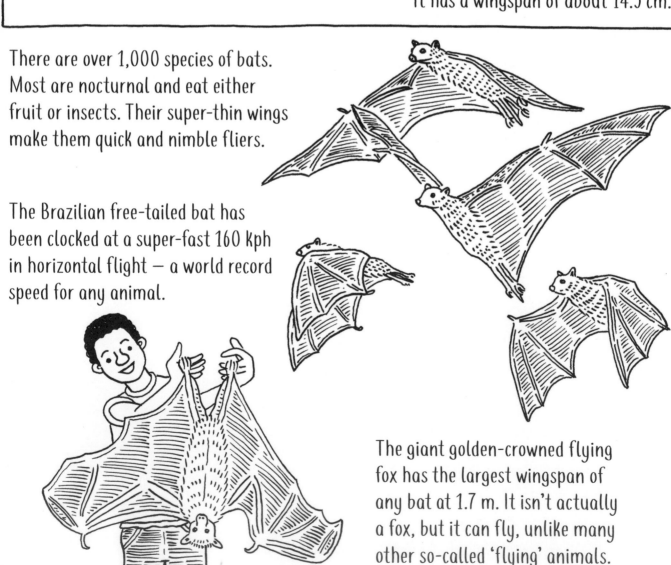

The giant golden-crowned flying fox has the largest wingspan of any bat at 1.7 m. It isn't actually a fox, but it can fly, unlike many other so-called 'flying' animals.

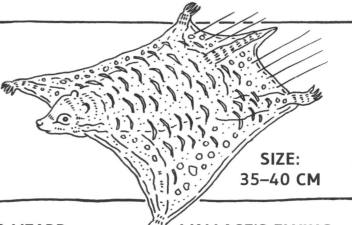

The colugo glides up to 70 m between forest trees in Southeast Asia. Like a bat, it uses a stretched, furry patagium to catch air. This rare creature is also called the 'flying lemur' — although it isn't a lemur, and it doesn't actually fly.

SIZE: 35–40 CM

FLYING SQUIRREL

SIZE: 25–37 CM

Flying squirrels glide between trees in many parts of the world.

DRACO LIZARD

SIZE: APPROX 20 CM

This type of Asian flying lizard glides between trees by extending its ribs to form a big, flat 'wing'.

WALLACE'S FLYING FROG

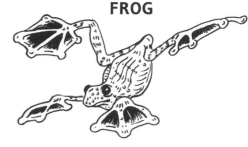

SIZE: 8–10 CM

The Wallace's flying frog glides to the floor in Asian forests using its huge webbed feet as if they were parachutes.

SIZE: UP TO 1.2 M

The flying snakes of Southeast Asia climb up trees and then throw themselves off branches into the air. The snakes flatten their bodies so that they can glide like wiggly Frisbees.

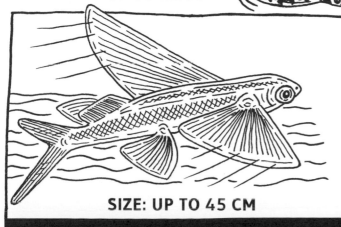

SIZE: UP TO 45 CM

Flying fish inhabit all the oceans of the world. Their 'wings' are specially adapted fins. They exit the water at high speed and can glide for up to 60 m, or longer if they catch an updraft, allowing them to escape predators like dolphins.

MAKE YOUR OWN COLUGO ON PAGE 51.
MAKE A FLYING FISH ON PAGE 53.

SPEEDY SEEDS

Many plants use the air to spread their seeds far and wide. Some of these seeds, such as sycamore seeds, spin, whirl or glide to stay airborne longer and travel further. Others, like dandelion seeds, drift in the wind like little parachutes.

MAPLE AND SYCAMORE TREES

Maple and sycamore trees produce winged seeds called 'samaras' that spiral as they fall. Scientists are studying their design and hope to produce a single-bladed helicopter rotor that works in a similar way.

THIS IS TWICE THE SIZE OF AN ACTUAL SEED.

THE SEED IS IN HERE

The whirling movement is called 'auto-gyration'.

COMMON DANDELION

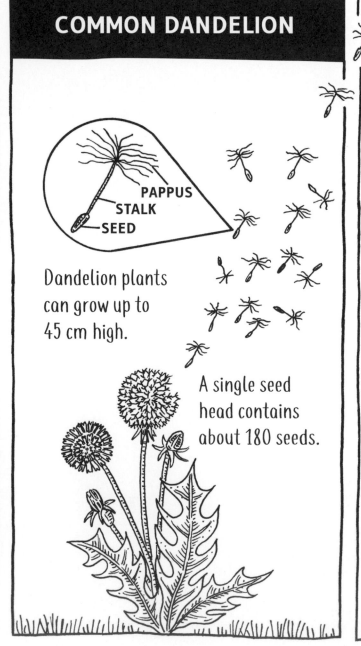

PAPPUS
STALK
SEED

Dandelion plants can grow up to 45 cm high.

A single seed head contains about 180 seeds.

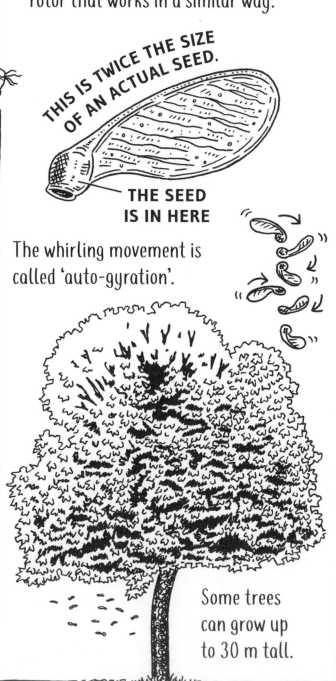

Some trees can grow up to 30 m tall.

WHIRLING NUT TREE

Also known as the helicopter tree or the propeller tree, the whirling nut tree produces bunches of amazing, winged seeds that twirl through the air as they fall.

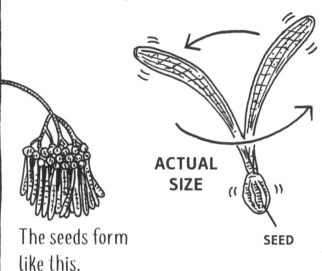

ACTUAL SIZE

SEED

The seeds form like this.

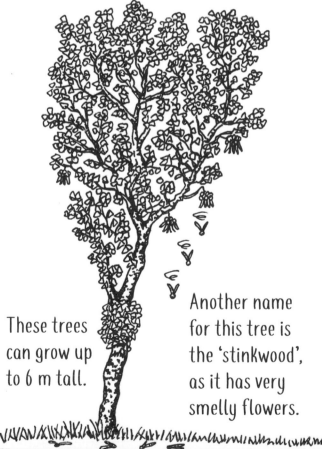

These trees can grow up to 6 m tall.

Another name for this tree is the 'stinkwood', as it has very smelly flowers.

JAVAN CUCUMBER

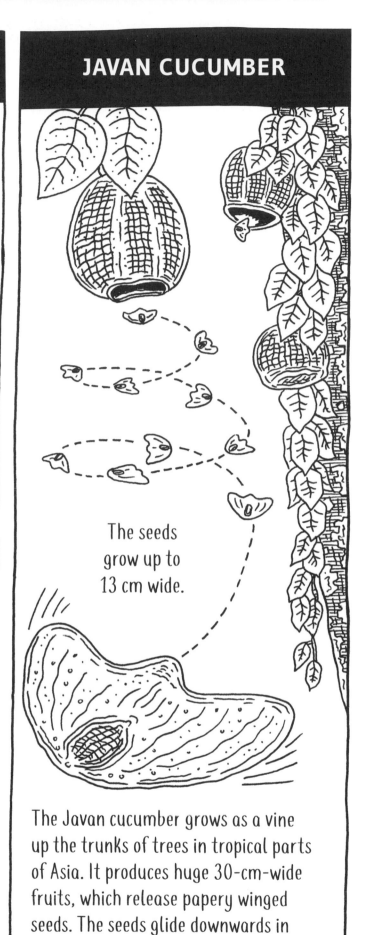

The seeds grow up to 13 cm wide.

The Javan cucumber grows as a vine up the trunks of trees in tropical parts of Asia. It produces huge 30-cm-wide fruits, which release papery winged seeds. The seeds glide downwards in slow, wide spirals.

MAKE TWO FLYING SEEDS ON PAGE 55.

FLYING LEGENDS

Modern humans have been around for about 300,000 years — and it seems they have dreamed of flying for almost as long. Here are some stories about human attempts at flight.

The most famous legend about an early attempt to fly is the ancient Greek legend of a clever inventor called Daedalus [day-da-lus] and his son, Icarus [ick-a-rus].

As punishment for a crime, they were imprisoned in a tall tower by the sea. The pair wanted to escape, so Daedalus made them each a pair of wings out of seagull feathers and wax. He warned Icarus to be careful and not to fly too high near the Sun or the wax would melt.

With the wings strapped to their arms, they flew from the tower like birds. In his excitement, Icarus ignored his father's warning and flew higher and higher, nearer to the Sun. Tragically, the wax on his wings melted and they fell apart, sending Icarus plummeting into the sea.

SQUAWK!

THE FALL OF ICARUS – FROM A 17TH-CENTURY ENGRAVING

British folk tales tell the story of King Bladud, who built a pair of wings over 2,000 years ago. According to the stories, Bladud used the wings to fly 100 km from the city of Bath to London. Sadly, on his arrival, Bladud is said to have crashed and died.

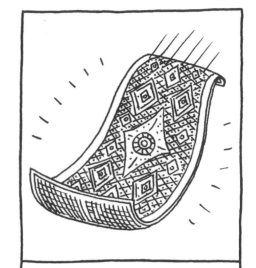

The Greek philosopher Archytas (are-kee-tas) is said to have made a wooden, steam-powered pigeon in about 400 BCE.

The collection of Middle Eastern tales known as *The One Thousand and One Nights* dates back to ancient times and features a magic flying carpet.

Boomerangs feature in the myths of the Indigenous people of Australia, stories which are at least 10,000 years old.

Boomerangs are the earliest heavier-than-air flying objects made by humans. They probably developed from flat sticks thrown by hunters to strike prey.

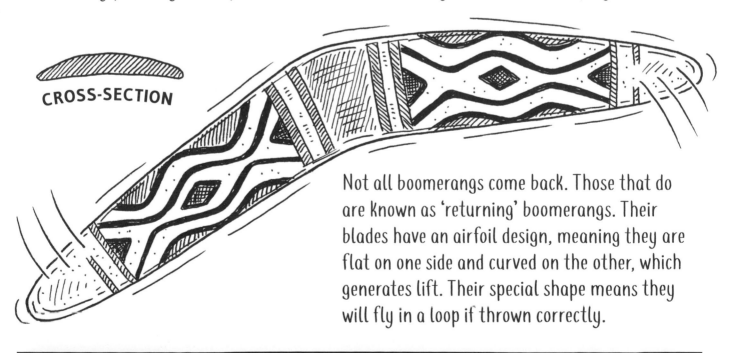

CROSS-SECTION

Not all boomerangs come back. Those that do are known as 'returning' boomerangs. Their blades have an airfoil design, meaning they are flat on one side and curved on the other, which generates lift. Their special shape means they will fly in a loop if thrown correctly.

MAKE A RETURNING BOOMERANG ON PAGE 57.

MADE IN CHINA

Without paper there could be no paper planes. Paper was invented in China nearly 2,000 years ago by a politician and inventor called Cai Lun [ky lun]. It is said that he invented it after noticing how wasps chewed wood into a pulp to make their papery nests.

CAI LUN (C. 48–121 CE)

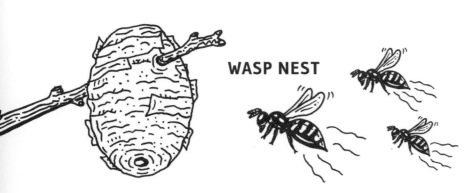

WASP NEST

Today, paper is named as one of the four great Chinese inventions, along with printing, gunpowder and the magnetic compass.

Papermaking spread rapidly across Asia. In Japan, the art of folding paper is called origami.

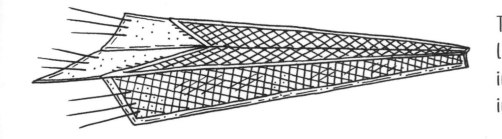

The first paper plane is likely to have been folded in China soon after the invention of paper.

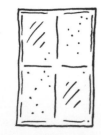

Paper is quite dense, making its weight a drag factor. However, it is strong. Air can't pass through it and it is easily bent or moulded, just like the aluminium sheeting used in aircraft today.

Al

ALUMINIUM

MAKE A CHINESE-STYLE PAPER PLANE (OR DRAGON DART) ON PAGE 59.

LU BAN
(C. 507–444 BCE)

MOZI
(C. 470–391 BCE)

The Chinese also invented the kite, about 2,500 years ago. Its invention is credited to two famous figures – an engineer called Lu Ban and a philosopher named Mozi.

Kites were originally rectangular and could be used to lift people into the air, often as a punishment.

Early kites were made from silk and bamboo. Kites were used by the Chinese military for signalling and measuring distances. Kite-making spread to Japan and beyond about 1,000 years later, thanks to Chinese missionaries.

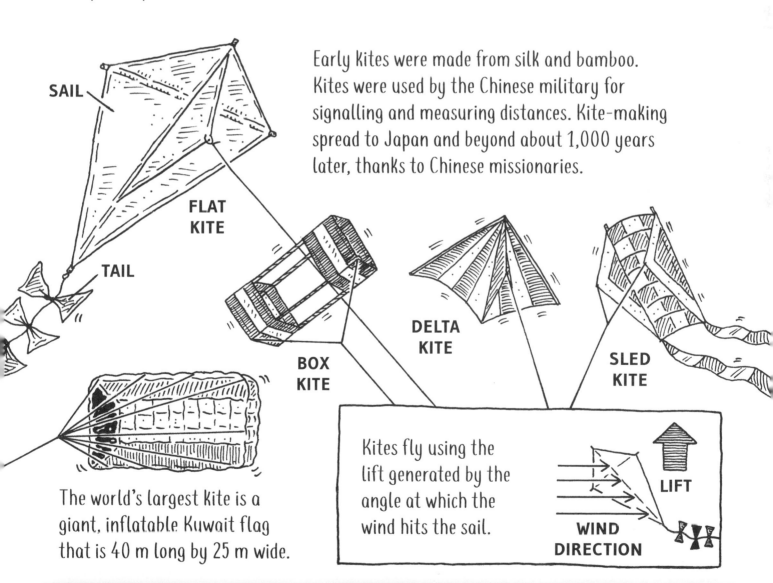

SAIL

FLAT KITE

TAIL

BOX KITE

DELTA KITE

SLED KITE

The world's largest kite is a giant, inflatable Kuwait flag that is 40 m long by 25 m wide.

Kites fly using the lift generated by the angle at which the wind hits the sail.

LIFT

WIND DIRECTION

MAKE A JAPANESE-STYLE KITE ON PAGE 61.

RECORD BREAKERS

You don't have to do something dangerous to be a world record breaker. This was proven by Japanese paper plane engineer Takuo Toda [tah-kew-oh toe-dah]. He created a paper plane that holds the world record for the longest time spent in the air. The plane stayed aloft for an amazing 29.2 seconds. Toda set the duration record in a sports stadium in Fukuyama City, in 2010.

RECORD HOLDER TAKUO TODA

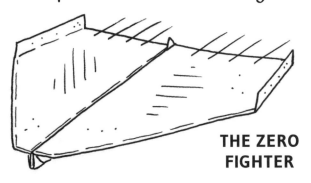

THE ZERO FIGHTER

Takuo Toda called his design the 'Zero Fighter'. It was just 10 cm long and made from a single, uncut sheet of light paper.

Think you could beat the record? Paper plane enthusiasts all want to break the 30 second barrier — why not give it a go?

JOHN M. COLLINS

The paper aeroplane distance record is held by Joe Ayoob and aircraft designer John M. Collins, who is also known as 'The Paper Airplane Guy'. On 26th February, 2012, their plane flew a massive 69.14 m at a Californian air base — that's almost three times the length of a tennis court.

JOHN NAMED HIS PLANE 'SUZANNE' AFTER HIS WIFE.

If you want to break the world record, you'll need an airworthy plane. The modern classic paper plane design, known as the 'Nakamura Lock', is a great model to begin your attempts.

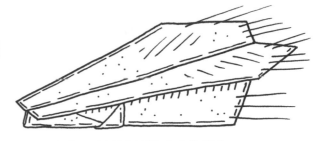

THE NAKAMURA LOCK

The Nakamura Lock is named after its inventor, Eiji Nakamura — a genius paper folder.

HERE'S HOW TO FOLD THE NAKAMURA LOCK USING A4 PAPER:

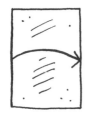

FOLD PAPER IN HALF LENGTHWAYS.

CREASE THE FOLD.

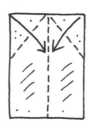

OPEN OUT AND FOLD TOP CORNERS TO CREASE.

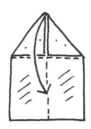

FOLD THE TOP SECTION DOWN AS SHOWN.

FOLD TOP CORNERS TO A SPOT 1–2 CM ABOVE THE POINT.

FOLD POINT UP TO 'LOCK' SIDES IN PLACE.

TURN MODEL OVER AND FOLD IN HALF.

FOLD SIDE 'A' TO SIDE 'B' TO FORM A WING.

DO THE SAME WITH THE OTHER SIDE.

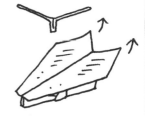

ANGLE THE WINGS AND CURL THE TIPS UP. NOW FLY YOUR PLANE!

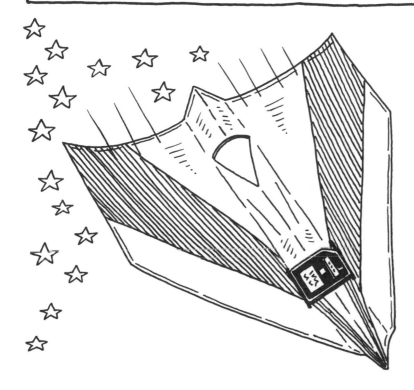

Another big event in paper plane history happened in 2011, when a small British team launched 200 paper planes from the edge of space, 37 km above Germany. The planes carried memory cards and some flew over 16,093.4 km back to Earth, flying as far as Australia.

THE PLANES WERE LAUNCHED FROM A WEATHER BALLOON.

BIRD BRAINS

Many early attempts to fly by humans were inspired by the Icarus story (see page 16). People strapped bird-like wings to their arms and then jumped off high towers. Most ended in broken bones, or worse — death. There are records of some of these early 'birdmen', but we have few actual facts, and some of the stories sound rather unbelievable.

The daredevil, Armen Firman [are-men fir-muhn], is said to have jumped off a tower in Córdoba, Spain in 852 CE. He wore a stiffened cloak that spread open and slowed his fall enough to survive.

Armen's fall is said to have been witnessed by Islamic inventor Abbas ibn Firnas [abb-bas bin fear-nas] (810–887 CE). In 875 CE, after studying birds for 20 years, Abbas also jumped from a tower in Córdoba, wearing wings made of vulture feathers and silk. It is claimed he flew a considerable distance but landed badly, hurting his back.

In 1010 CE, an English monk, called Eilmer of Malmesbury, is said to have jumped from a tower and flown for 15 seconds, but unfortunately broke both legs on landing.

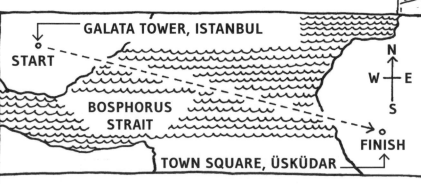

GALATA TOWER, ISTANBUL
START
N
W — E
S
BOSPHORUS
STRAIT
FINISH
TOWN SQUARE, ÜSKÜDAR

In 1638 CE, pioneering aviator Hezârfen Ahmet Çelebi [hez-are-fen ah-met chi-lee-bee] jumped from a tower, wearing eagle wings. It is said he managed to fly 3.35 km across the Bosphorus strait.

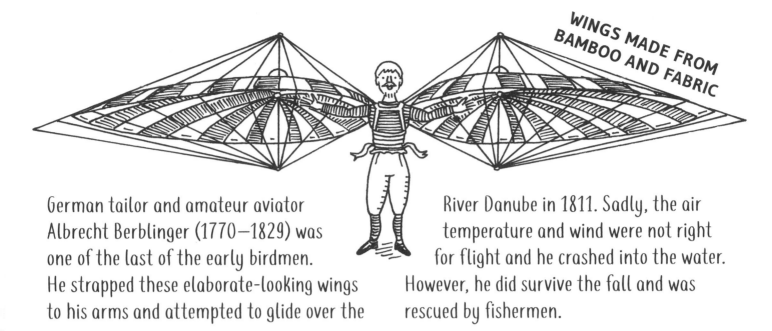

WINGS MADE FROM BAMBOO AND FABRIC

German tailor and amateur aviator Albrecht Berblinger (1770–1829) was one of the last of the early birdmen. He strapped these elaborate-looking wings to his arms and attempted to glide over the River Danube in 1811. Sadly, the air temperature and wind were not right for flight and he crashed into the water. However, he did survive the fall and was rescued by fishermen.

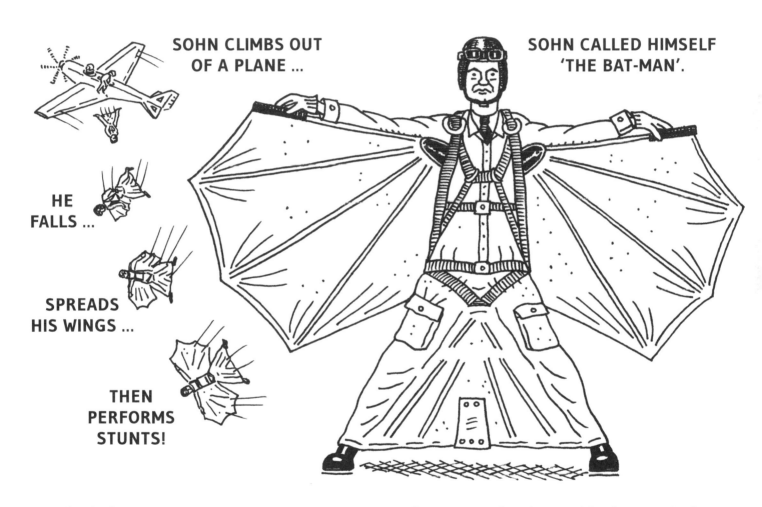

SOHN CLIMBS OUT OF A PLANE ...

HE FALLS ...

SPREADS HIS WINGS ...

THEN PERFORMS STUNTS!

SOHN CALLED HIMSELF 'THE BAT-MAN'.

In the 20th century, birdmen were reborn as daredevils once again. American carnival stuntman Clem Sohn (1910–1937) took to jumping out of planes at a height of about 3,000 m in a winged suit. To the amazement of audiences, he glided at high speed before opening a parachute and floating safely down to the ground. Tragically, Sohn died at an airshow in 1937 when his parachute failed to open properly.

MAKE YOUR OWN CLEM SOHN ON PAGE 63.

IN A FLAP

LEONARDO DA VINCI (1452–1519)

Instead of simply attaching wings to their arms, some people tried making flying machines. The notebooks of Italian genius Leonardo da Vinci contain sketches for various flying machines, including a man-powered ornithopter (an aircraft with flapping wings) that was operated with levers and pulleys.

SOME OF DA VINCI'S DESIGNS

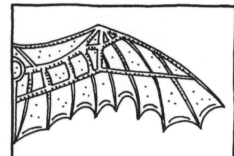

WING DESIGN C. 1485

ORNITHOPTER DESIGN C. 1487

MODERN REPLICA

It is uncertain whether da Vinci actually made a trial version of his ornithopter design, but experts today think it would never have got off the ground — it is unlikely that a human could generate enough power.

People have continued to experiment with ornithopters over the centuries. Working versions have been made using engines, but no one has yet made a solely human-powered model.

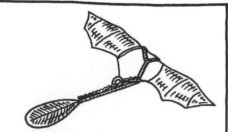

RUBBER BAND POWERED FLAPPING TOY (1872)

MODERN FLAPPING BIRD TOY

TEST AIRCRAFT (1999)

UP, UP AND AWAY

In China, around the year 280 BCE, sky lanterns were used by the military to carry messages. Their simple design was later used as inspiration for the hot-air balloon.

SKY LANTERN MADE FROM WIRE AND PAPER

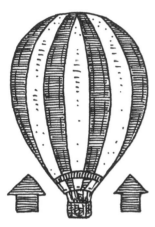

Hot-air balloons rise upwards because the warm air inside them is less dense (and therefore lighter) than the air outside. This generates lift causing the balloon to rise upwards, just like a cork floating on water.

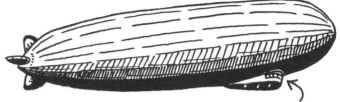

A ZEPPELIN   **GONDOLA WITH PASSENGERS**

Lightweight gases such as helium and hydrogen can also be used in the envelopes (large balloon parts) of hot-air balloons and airships, such as the famous zeppelins of 100 years ago.

IT FLEW 8.8 KM BEFORE LANDING.   **IT WAS IN THE AIR FOR 25 MINUTES.**

The first untethered manned flight in a hot-air balloon took place in France on the 21st November, 1783. The balloon was designed by the Montgolfier brothers, Joseph-Michel and Jacques-Étienne.

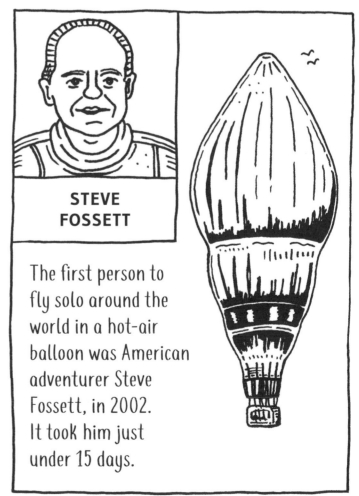

STEVE FOSSETT

The first person to fly solo around the world in a hot-air balloon was American adventurer Steve Fossett, in 2002. It took him just under 15 days.

AVID AVIATORS

**SIR GEORGE CAYLEY
(1773–1857)**

In the 19th century, two people made amazing advances in aviation. The first was Sir George Cayley, a wealthy man from Yorkshire, England. Often called 'The Father of Aviation', Cayley designed the first glider strong enough to carry an adult.

Cayley was fascinated with flight from childhood and was the first to recognize the four forces that act on an aircraft — drag, weight, lift and thrust (see page 5).

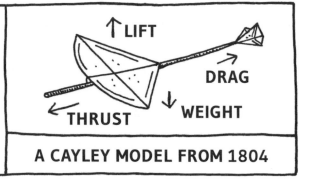

↑ LIFT

DRAG

← THRUST   ↓ WEIGHT

A CAYLEY MODEL FROM 1804

Cayley designed and tested many flying machines in his life. In the summer of 1853, he persuaded his coachman to pilot his latest glider down a hill in front of his home and into the air. It flew for around 200 m and made history in the process.

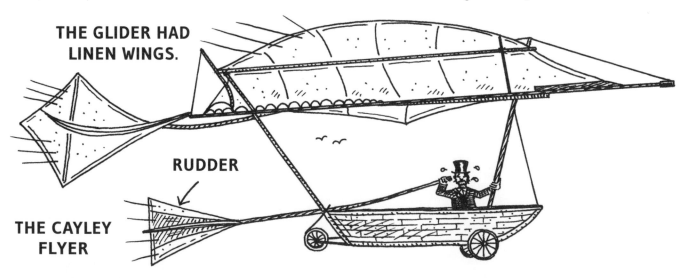

**THE GLIDER HAD
LINEN WINGS.**

RUDDER

**THE CAYLEY
FLYER**

Cayley called his glider a 'Navigable Parachute', because it could be steered. After it crash-landed, the coachman quit, saying "I was hired to drive, not fly!"

MAKE THE CAYLEY GLIDER ON PAGE 65.

**OTTO LILIENTHAL
(1848–1896)**

The second great figure was German engineer and aviator Otto Lilienthal [lilli-en-tarl]. Like George Cayley, Lilienthal was obsessed with flight as a child. He studied how different birds flew and even made himself a pair of strap-on wings, which unfortunately didn't work.

After training as an engineer, Lilienthal developed a series of flying machines, which closely resembled modern hang-gliders. Launched from a specially built, artificial hill, Lilienthal flew them himself, using his body weight to steer them.

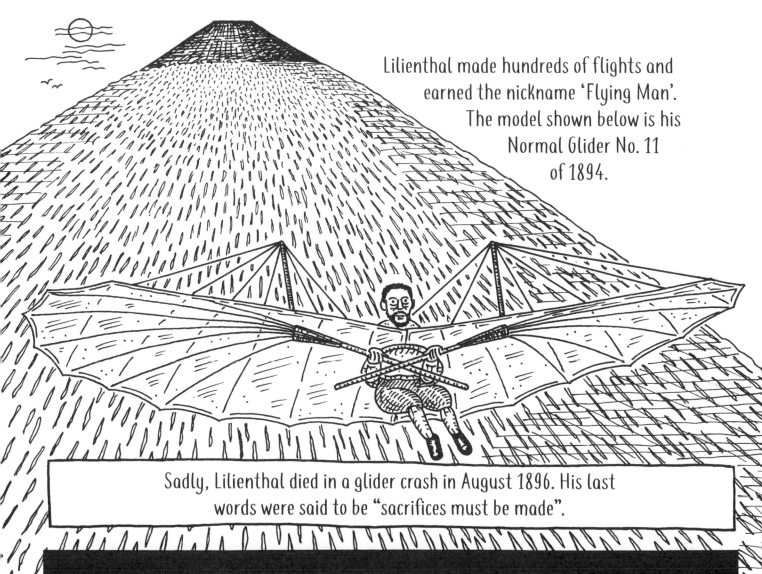

Lilienthal made hundreds of flights and earned the nickname 'Flying Man'. The model shown below is his Normal Glider No. 11 of 1894.

Sadly, Lilienthal died in a glider crash in August 1896. His last words were said to be "sacrifices must be made".

MAKE A LILIENTHAL GLIDER ON PAGE 67.

THE WRIGHT STUFF

The death of Otto Lilienthal (see page 27) made newspaper headlines around the world. In America, the shocking news changed the lives of two young bicycle makers, Orville Wright and his brother Wilbur.

ORVILLE (1871–1948)

WILBUR (1867–1912)

A WRIGHT GLIDER OF 1901

In 1900, the brothers began to experiment with their own glider models at Kitty Hawk, North Carolina. It was an area known for its sandy plains and strong winds — perfect for testing flying machines.

Over the next few years, they moved ever closer to their goal of building the world's first powered, heavier-than-air machine, capable of sustained and controllable flight. Their experiments resulted in the Wright Flyer I. But would it work?

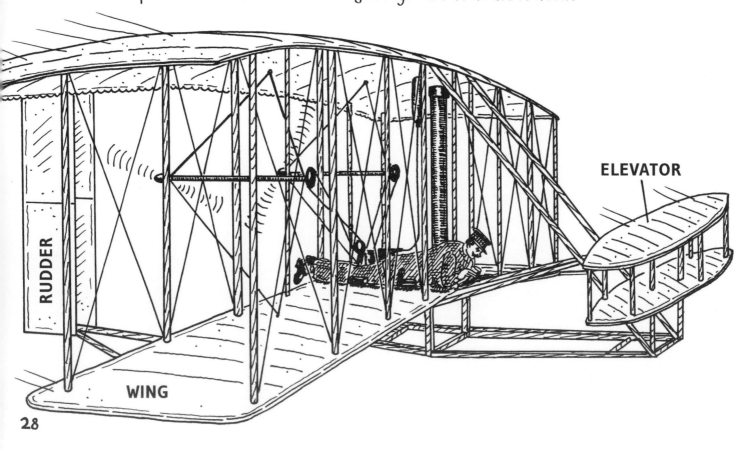

ELEVATOR

RUDDER

WING

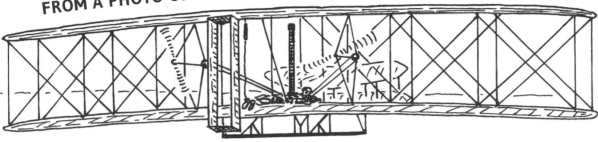

FROM A PHOTO OF THE ACTUAL FLIGHT

WILBUR RAN BEHIND THE FLYER.

↙ **LAUNCH RAIL**

At 10:35 am on 17th December, 1903, the Wright Flyer I sped down a short launch rail and lifted into the air. Powered by a small petrol engine and piloted by Orville, the flyer flew 36.6 m before touching down.

The entire flight lasted just 12 seconds — about as long as it takes to read the above description out loud. But it changed the history of flight forever.

The Wright Flyer I may look strange to us today, but it had all the essential elements of a modern aeroplane — wings, elevators, a rudder and an engine generating both lift and thrust. It was called a 'bi-plane' because it had two sets of wings, one positioned on top of the other.

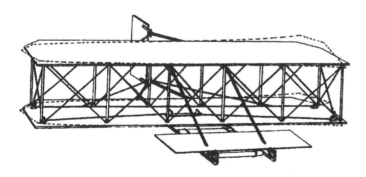

A SKETCH FROM THE PATENT DOCUMENT

The brothers patented (made it so that no one could copy) their invention, set up a company and spread flying across the world. The aviation age had begun!

Amazingly, a piece of wing cloth and a small bit of wood from the Wright Flyer I were taken to the Moon in 1969, by the first humans to ever walk on the lunar surface.

MAKE A MINI WRIGHT FLYER I ON PAGE 69.

THE FLYING FRENCHMAN

The Wright Brothers' success inspired many rival inventors. In 1906, Romanian Traian Vuia [try-ann voo-yah], managed a short flight of 11 m in a monoplane – a plane with just one set of wings. However, far more successful was French businessman and inventor, Louis Blériot [loo-ee blair-ee-oh].

LOUIS BLÉRIOT (1872–1936)

Blériot used his wealth to build a succession of aeroplanes, including his most famous design, the Blériot XI – a monoplane.

THE BLÉRIOT XI

BLÉRIOT ABOVE THE ENGLISH CHANNEL

A British newspaper had offered a prize of £1,000 to the first aeroplane to fly over the English Channel, the stretch of sea between England and France. Blériot was up for the challenge.

At 4:41 am on 25th July, 1909, Blériot took off from France in his Blériot XI and headed for England. Flying at 72 kph, Blériot was in the air for just over 36 minutes. After flying 35.4 km over the Channel he landed with a bump in Dover. The precise landing spot was outlined in bricks as a memorial to the first international plane flight.

THE MEMORIAL IN DOVER

AFTER MAKING THE FIRST CHANNEL FLIGHT BY AEROPLANE, LOUIS BLÉRIOT LANDED AT THIS SPOT ON SUNDAY 25TH JULY, 1909

The world went plane crazy and, in the years after Blériot's flight, many great aviators and famous fliers took to the skies.

In 1927, American pilot Charles Lindbergh (1902–1974) became world famous for the first solo, non-stop transatlantic (over the Atlantic Ocean) flight between New York and Paris. The public called him 'Lucky Lindy'.

American aviatrix Amelia Earheart (1897–1937) was the first woman to fly across the Atlantic Ocean on 20th May, 1932. She landed in Ireland where a farm worker asked her "Have you come far?"

Bessie Coleman (1892–1926) was the first African-American woman to hold a pilot's licence, though she had to go to France to get it. Bessie said, "The air is the only place free from prejudices."

English flier Amy Johnson (1903–1941) made history as the first woman pilot to fly alone from England to Australia in 1930. The flight took 19 days and she became so famous that songs were written about her.

American test pilot Chuck Yeager (born 1923) made history as the first person to fly faster than the speed of sound (see page 38) in a rocket-powered Bell X-1 plane nicknamed *Glamorous Glennis* on 14th October, 1947.

MAKE A MODEL BLÉRIOT XI MONOPLANE ON PAGE 71.

TAKE CONTROL

Although there have been great advances in the world of aviation, modern planes still have much in common with those of the past. Amelia Earhart's bright red Lockheed Vega 5B of 1932 had the same parts as those that allow planes to manoeuvre in the air nowadays. Here are some of the useful plane parts and how they work:

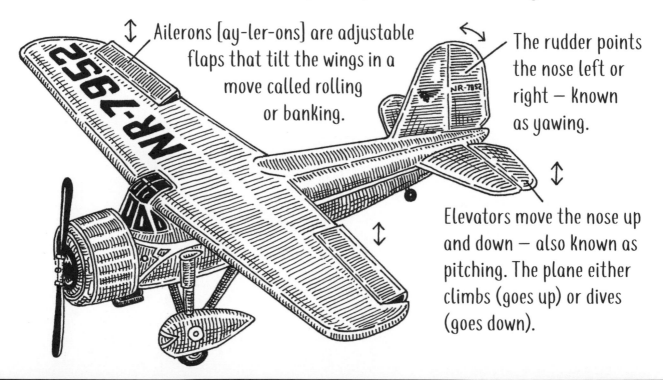

Ailerons (ay-ler-ons) are adjustable flaps that tilt the wings in a move called rolling or banking.

The rudder points the nose left or right — known as yawing.

Elevators move the nose up and down — also known as pitching. The plane either climbs (goes up) or dives (goes down).

YOU CAN ALSO CONTROL YOUR MODELS BY MAKING A FEW SMALL ADJUSTMENTS:

TIPS UP
PLANE FLIES UP
Bent like this, a model will pitch upwards in the air.

TIPS DOWN
PLANE FLIES DOWN
Bent like this, a model will pitch downwards in the air.

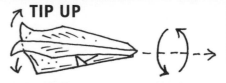

TIP UP
TIP DOWN PLANE ROLLS
Bent like this, a model will roll as it flies forwards.

The angle at which a plane or model hits the air is very important. If it is too steep, it will stall (stop) and then dive down.

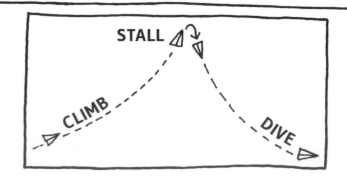

STALL

CLIMB

DIVE

SPINNING WINGS

Helicopters are aircraft that use spinning rotor blades to produce lift and thrust. The blades have an airfoil cross-section, just like a wing.

SOME CRAFT CAN HAVE SEVEN OR MORE BLADES.

BLADE CROSS-SECTION

TOP VIEW OF A ROTOR

Unlike most planes, helicopters can fly vertically up and down, which means that they do not need a runway to take off from. They can also fly sideways and backwards and even hover in one place.

The word 'helicopter' means 'spiral wing' and was coined by French inventor Gustave Ponton d'Amécourt [goo-stav pon-ton dam-eh-cour] (1825–1888). Sadly, his attempts to produce a working steam-powered model failed.

GUSTAV IN 1863

The modern helicopter was largely developed by engineer Igor Sikorsky (1889–1972) in the 1940s. Today the world's largest helicopter is the Russian Mil Mi-26. It has eight rotor blades and is capable of lifting the weight of two African elephants.

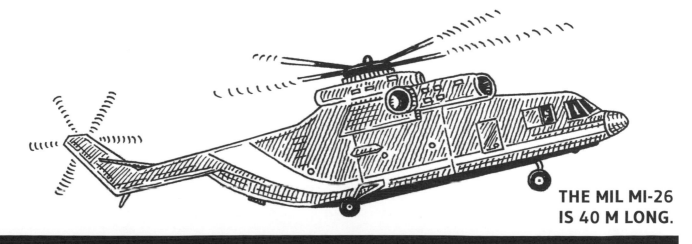

THE MIL MI-26 IS 40 M LONG.

MAKE A PAIR OF HELICOPTER BLADES ON PAGE 73.

READY, JET ... GO!

The first planes used piston engines, like those in a car, to drive propellers. However, the invention of the far more powerful jet engine in 1930 changed flying forever. Jet engines use hot exhaust gases to power an aircraft in flight.

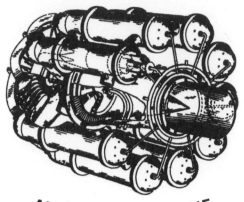

AN EARLY JET ENGINE

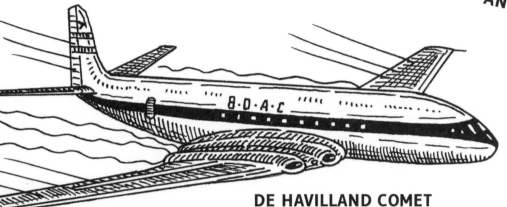

DE HAVILLAND COMET JETLINER, 1952

The world's first passenger jet service launched in Great Britain in 1952. Passengers were known as 'The Jet Set'.

Early jet planes could carry approximately 40 passengers. Today, the world's largest passenger jet – the Airbus A380 – can carry over 850 passengers plus flight crew.

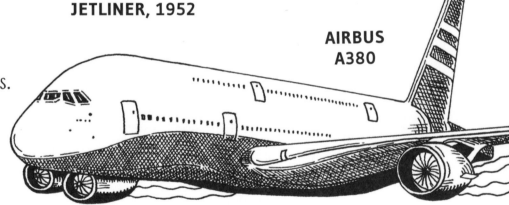

AIRBUS A380

THE A380 IS A DOUBLE-DECKER JET WITH PASSENGERS SEATED ON TWO LEVELS.

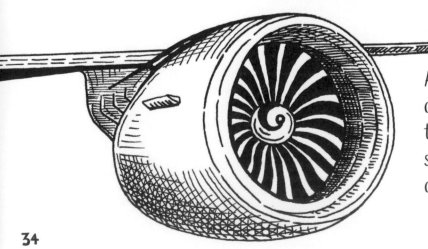

A typical jet engine burns 4.5 litres of aviation fuel every second. Two engines together can push a passenger jet at speeds in excess of 800 kph but are also very noisy and polluting.

FLYING FOR FUN

Hang-gliding has come a long way since the days of Otto Lilienthal (see page 27). Now, it's a common hobby for many flying enthusiasts and thrill-seekers.

You steer a hang-glider by shifting your weight.

Microlights are a form of powered hang-glider with a small cockpit.

Paragliders launch off cliffs under a giant kite sail.

MAKE A HANG-GLIDER ON PAGE 75.

SUPER SONIC

Concorde was a joint British-French supersonic jet that operated from 1976 to 2003. It flew passengers across the globe at speeds of 2,179 kph!

The speed of sound is known as 'Mach 1'. Concorde could reach 'Mach 2' (twice as fast as the speed of sound).

THE WINGS WERE 'DELTA'-SHAPED (OR TRIANGLE-SHAPED) TO REDUCE DRAG.

CONCORDE MACHMETER

'Supersonic' means that something can travel through the air faster than sound does.

Whenever Concorde passed the sound barrier it created a very noisy shock wave, known as a ...

SONIC BOOM!

THE NAME 'DELTA' COMES FROM THE GREEK LETTER (Δ), WHICH IS SHAPED LIKE A TRIANGLE.

CONCORDE CRUISED AT NEARLY 20 KM ABOVE EARTH.

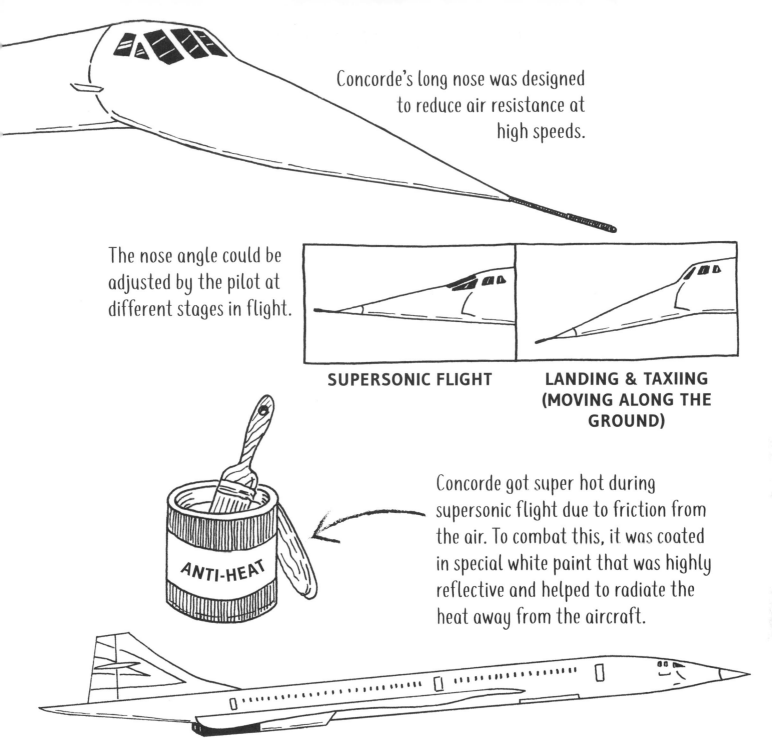

Concorde's long nose was designed to reduce air resistance at high speeds.

The nose angle could be adjusted by the pilot at different stages in flight.

SUPERSONIC FLIGHT

LANDING & TAXIING (MOVING ALONG THE GROUND)

Concorde got super hot during supersonic flight due to friction from the air. To combat this, it was coated in special white paint that was highly reflective and helped to radiate the heat away from the aircraft.

ANTI-HEAT

Concorde was just over 62 m long, but stretched up to 25 cm longer in supersonic flight, due to the heating of its frame. This means it grew by roughly the same amount as the length of the model Concorde on page 77.

Concorde was retired in 2003 due to rising costs and concerns about safety and noise pollution. However, some wealthy fans have plans to buy one and get it flying again.

RELAUNCH YOUR OWN CONCORDE ON PAGE 77.

ROCKET SCIENCE

Rockets were invented in China about 1,000 years ago, probably right after gunpowder was invented. Gunpowder ignites to produce hot gases that expand rapidly and can propel a rocket high into the air.

AN EARLY CHINESE 'FIRE ARROW' OR ROCKET

One Chinese legend tells of a court official called Wan Hu, who tied himself to a chair that had 47 lit fireworks attached to it. He held two kites and hoped that the fireworks would propel him upwards so that he could fly into space. Sadly, instead he simply exploded (don't try this at home!).

For hundreds of years, rockets were mostly used to wage war and destruction. However, in 1947, Chuck Yeager became the first person to break the sound barrier in a rocket-powered experimental Bell X-1 plane (see page 31).

APOLLO II MISSION BADGE

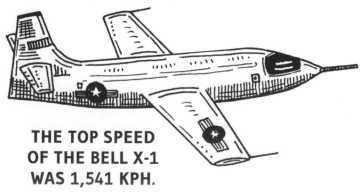

THE TOP SPEED OF THE BELL X-1 WAS 1,541 KPH.

Today, rockets are often associated with space flight. Rockets were used to send the cosmonaut Yuri Gagarin (1934–1968) into space for the first manned orbit of Earth in 1961. They were also used for the first manned Moon landing by the Apollo Mission in 1969.

Most rockets can only be used once, but the space shuttle fleet was an exception to the rule. Developed by the American space organization NASA, the space shuttles were re-usable spacecraft that were launched into orbit around Earth on the back of a massive fuel tank and two powerful booster rockets.

The first shuttle, *Enterprise*, only worked in Earth's atmosphere, but the later shuttles, *Columbia*, *Challenger*, *Discovery*, *Atlantis* and *Endeavour*, were space-worthy orbiters. They were used to deliver satellites and people into space, to conduct research and build the International Space Station.

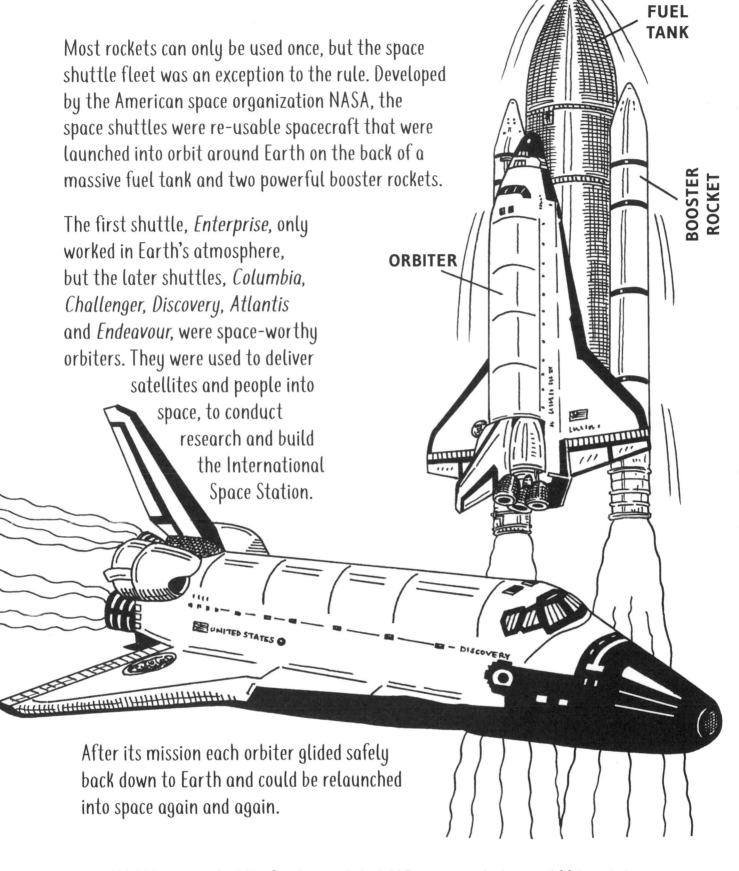

FUEL TANK

BOOSTER ROCKET

ORBITER

UNITED STATES

DISCOVERY

After its mission each orbiter glided safely back down to Earth and could be relaunched into space again and again.

NASA's space shuttle fleet completed 135 missions between 1981 and its retirement in 2011 — clocking up more than 872 million km between them.

MAKE A SPACE SHUTTLE ON PAGE 79.

BACK TO THE FUTURE

After millions of years of flight on this planet — from insects to astronauts — who knows how flight will advance in the future.

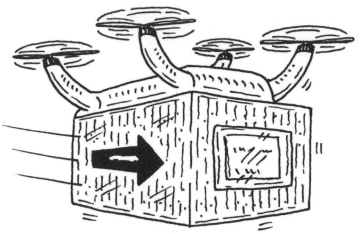

Already roaming the skies are drones — small, steerable model helicopters. Popular as toys, they are currently being tested as a way of delivering things to your home.

The dream of flying with a jet-pack on your back is an old one that is now a reality. However, modern jet-packs only work for up to 17 minutes and currently cost over £390,000!

JET-PACK SUIT FROM A SCI-FI BOOK OF 1928

THIS MODEL FLYING CAR CAN FLY AT 96.5 KPH.

Finally, how about heading off to school in a flying car, just like Harry Potter? Several working prototypes already exist and, scarily, you don't even need a pilot's licence to fly one.

Now it's time to make and fly your own models. Carefully read all of the instructions for each model before you begin cutting. Cut along the solid lines and fold along the dashed lines on the model pieces. Try to have a steady hand when cutting so that you don't cut through any of the instructions. Most of all, have fun, and remember: when it comes to flying, the sky is no longer the limit!

MEGANEURA

Follow the steps to make this model:

- Cut along all the solid outlines
- Fold along the dotted lines
- Apply glue to all the green areas marked GLUE

FOLD AND GLUE THE WINGS TOGETHER

CUT DOWN HERE

CUT DOWN HERE

BODY AND WINGS

GLUE THESE SIDES TOGETHER

GLUE THESE SIDES TOGETHER

TOP PIECE

1 Fold the first set of wings under and glue to the second set.

2 Fold and glue the body together.

3 Glue the top piece on to the body.

4 Gently bend up the tips of the wings.

ADD PAPERCLIPS TO THE NOSE

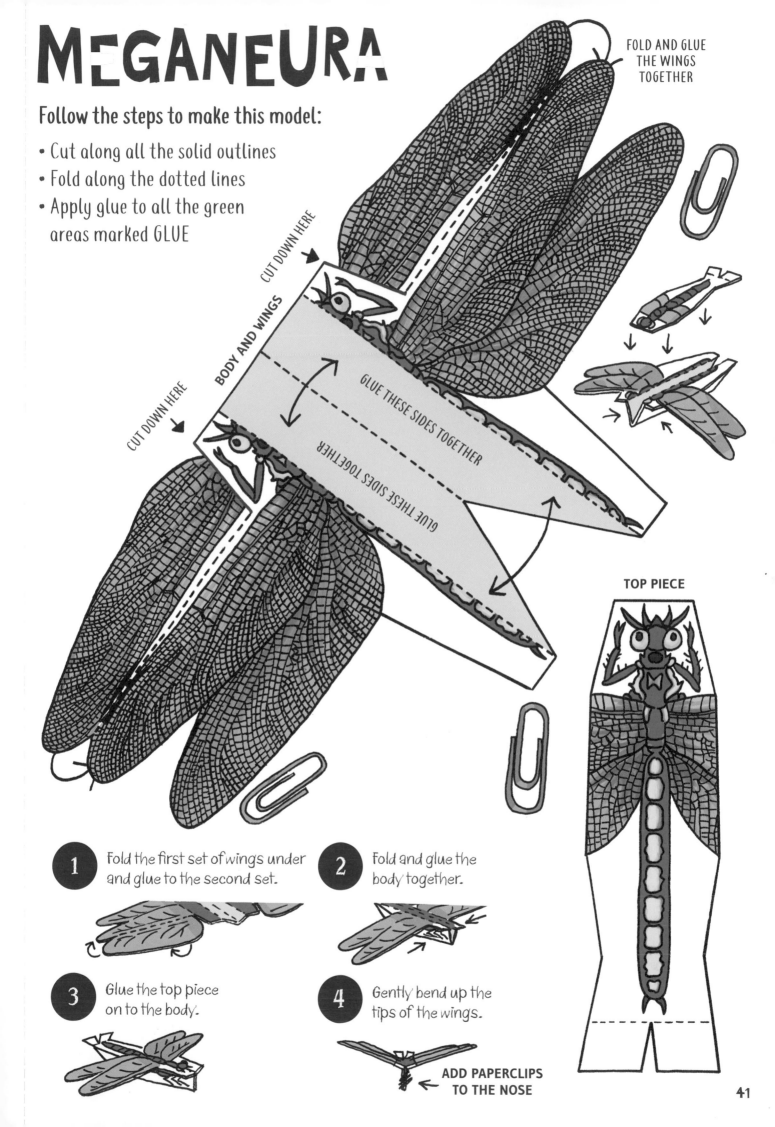

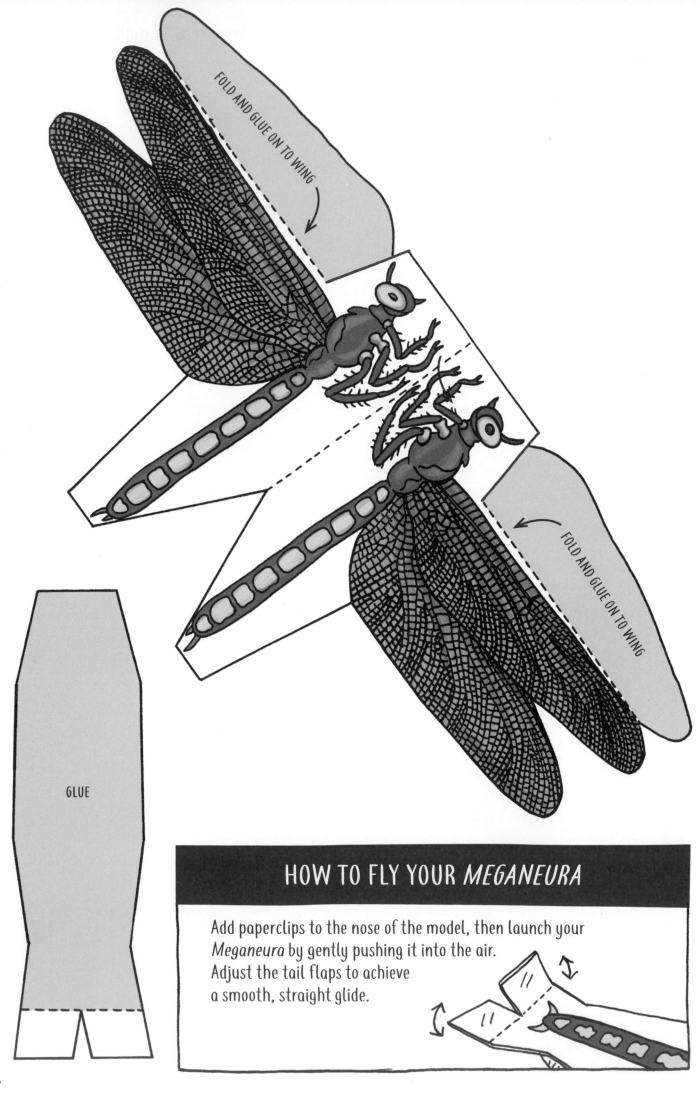

FOLD AND GLUE ON TO WING

FOLD AND GLUE ON TO WING

GLUE

HOW TO FLY YOUR *MEGANEURA*

Add paperclips to the nose of the model, then launch your *Meganeura* by gently pushing it into the air. Adjust the tail flaps to achieve a smooth, straight glide.

MONARCH BUTTERFLY

Follow the steps to make this model:

- Cut along all the solid outlines
- Fold along the dotted lines
- Apply glue to all the green areas marked GLUE

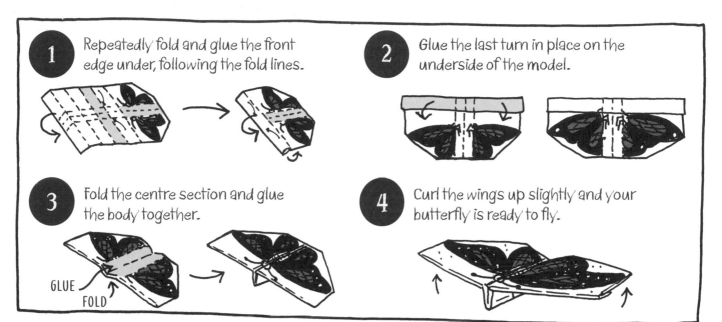

1. Repeatedly fold and glue the front edge under, following the fold lines.

2. Glue the last turn in place on the underside of the model.

3. Fold the centre section and glue the body together.
   GLUE
   FOLD

4. Curl the wings up slightly and your butterfly is ready to fly.

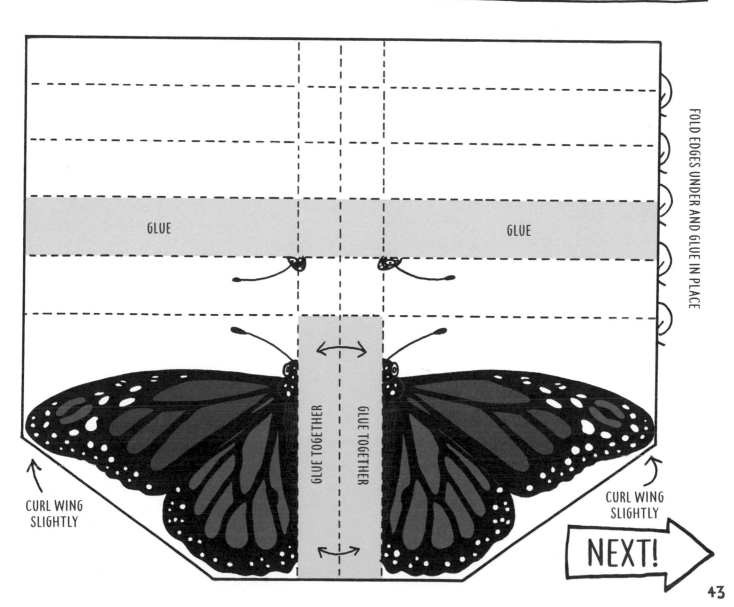

GLUE

GLUE

FOLD EDGES UNDER AND GLUE IN PLACE

GLUE TOGETHER

GLUE TOGETHER

CURL WING SLIGHTLY

CURL WING SLIGHTLY

NEXT!

HOW TO FLY YOUR BUTTERFLY

Gently push the model into the air.
What happens if you throw it harder?

Curl the corners of the wings up or down
to adjust the flight.

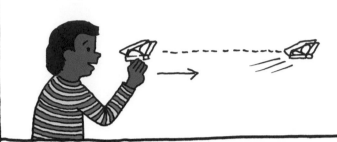

Have a go at experimenting with changing the angle of the wings.
Here are some angles you could try:

TYPICAL
(raised shallow angle)

HORIZONTAL
(no angle)

STEEP
(increased raised angle)

LOWERED
(low shallow angle)

FOLD OVER AND GLUE

FOLD OVER AND GLUE

FOLD OVER AND GLUE

FOLD OVER AND GLUE

FOLD OVER AND GLUE

GLUE FINAL FOLD HERE

FOLD OVER AND GLUE

FOLD OVER AND GLUE

FOLD OVER AND GLUE

FOLD OVER AND GLUE

FOLD OVER AND GLUE

GLUE FINAL FOLD HERE

ARCHAEOPTERYX

Follow the steps to make this model:

- Cut along all the solid outlines
- Fold along the dotted lines
- Apply glue to all the green areas marked GLUE

1 Cut out the body and wing pieces. On the body piece, cut down the solid red lines to separate the head tabs.

2 Turn the body over. Fold and glue the tabs inside the head.

WING PIECE

3 Fold and glue the body closed and fold down the wings.

4 Glue the body piece on top of the wing piece, leaving the tabs sticking out.

CUT

GLUE

GLUE

GLUE GLUE

5 Fold the tabs on the wing piece over and glue in place.

GLUE

GLUE

CUT

BODY PIECE

DONE!

TIME TO FLY!

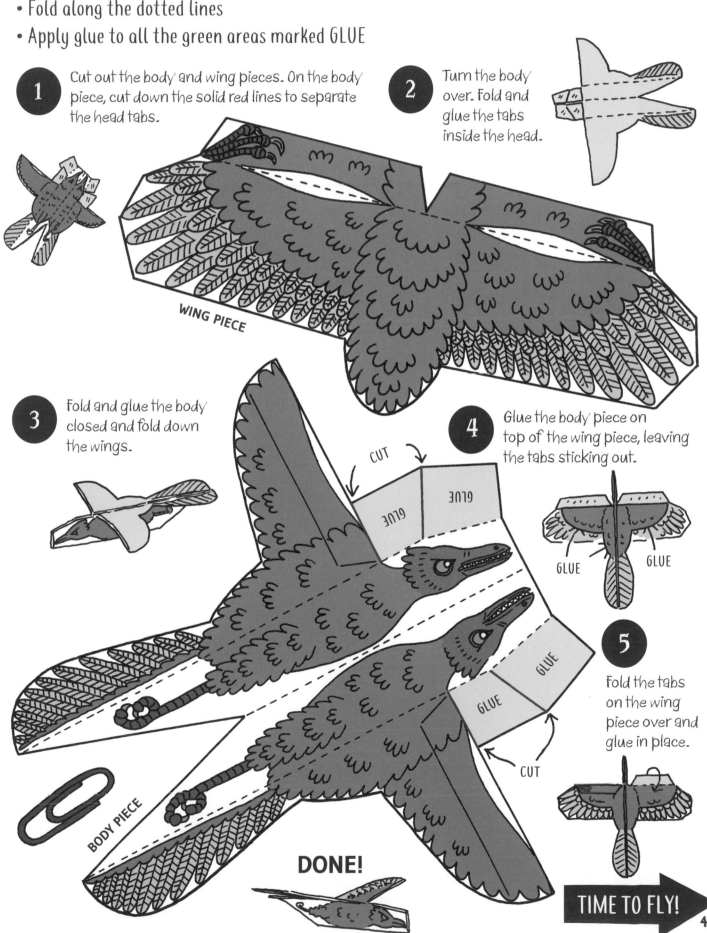

HOW TO FLY YOUR *ARCHAEOPTERYX*

Add one or more paperclips to the head.

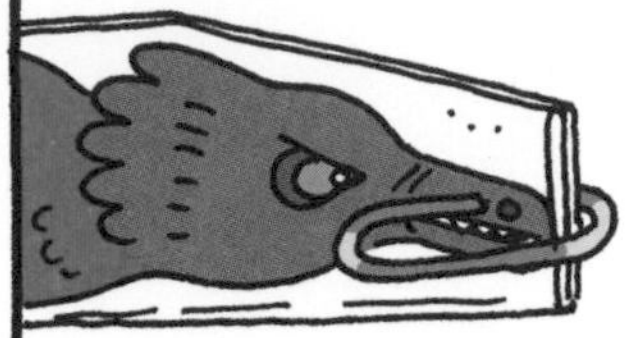

Angle the wings – experiment with different degrees.

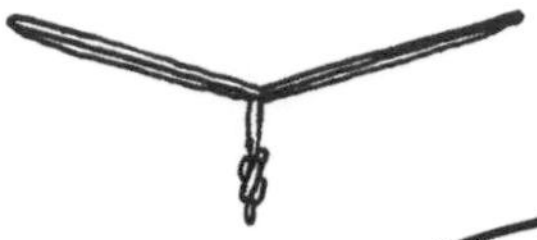

Launch smoothly into the air.

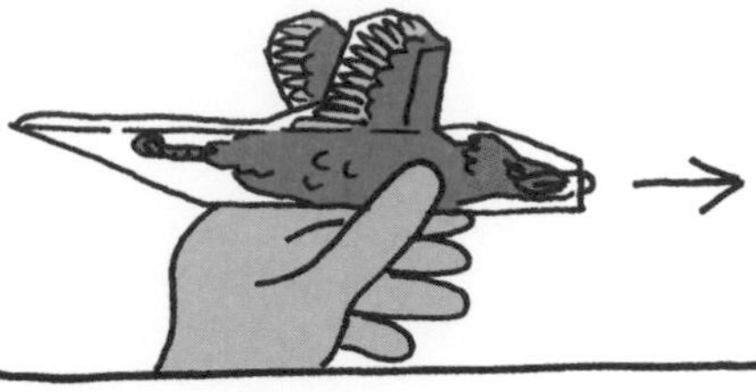

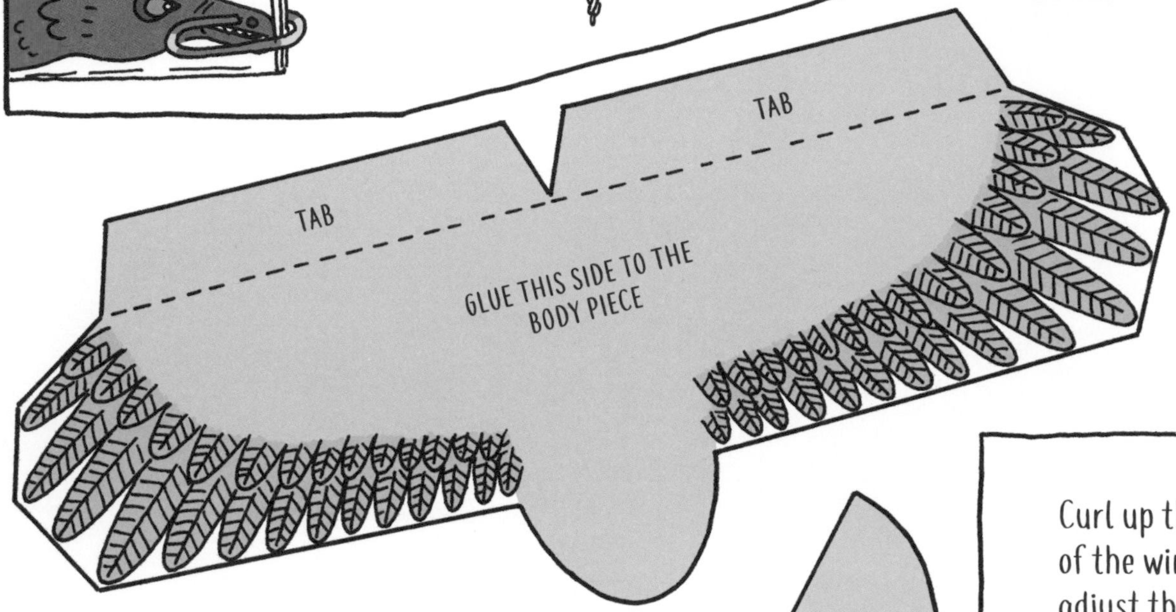
TAB
TAB
GLUE THIS SIDE TO THE BODY PIECE

Curl up the tips of the wings to adjust the flight.

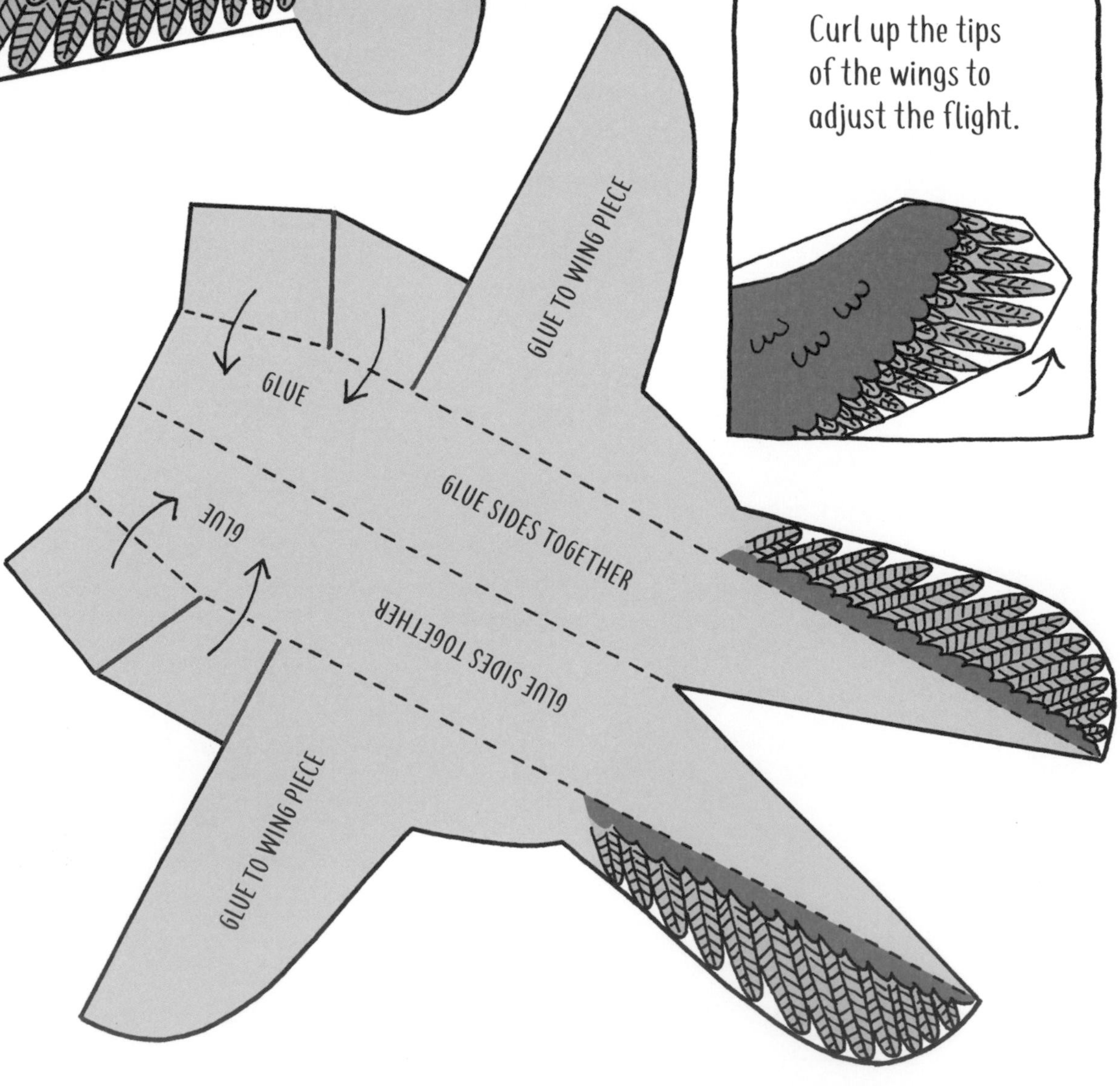
GLUE TO WING PIECE
GLUE
GLUE SIDES TOGETHER
GLUE
GLUE SIDES TOGETHER
GLUE TO WING PIECE

GOLDEN EAGLE

Follow the steps to make this model:

- Cut along all the solid outlines
- Fold along the dotted lines
- Apply glue to all the green areas marked GLUE

1 Start this way up.

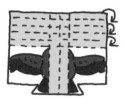

2 Fold and glue the paper over, following the fold lines.

3 You will be left with a thick strip – glue this down.

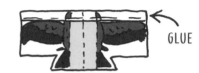

GLUE

4 Fold the model in half. Then fold down the wings.

5 Glue the body together.

DONE!

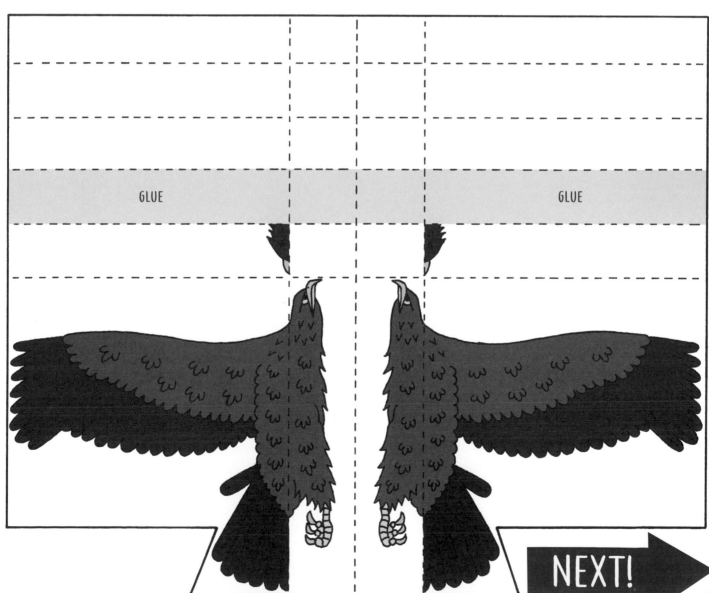

GLUE

GLUE

NEXT!

HOW TO FLY YOUR EAGLE

This model is best flown outdoors or in a large indoor space.
It should not require any extra weight on the nose.

Before you launch it, curl up
the edges of the wings and tail.

Throw the model with force up into the air.
If you're outside, throw it into the wind.

With practice and adjustment, the model can do loops, rolls, circles and smooth glides.
Experiment with the angle of the wings to achieve these stunts.

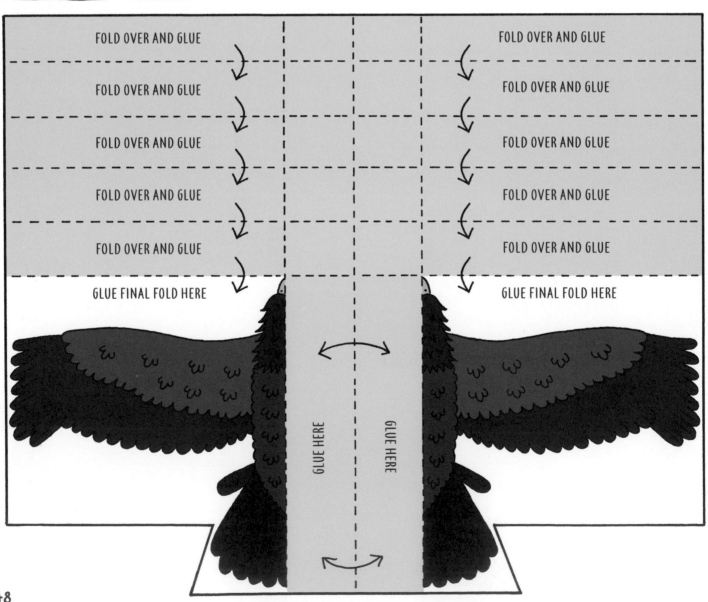

48

KINGFISHER

Follow the steps to make this model:

- Cut along all the solid outlines
- Fold along the dotted lines
- Apply glue to all the green areas marked GLUE

1 Fold and glue the head and beak on both sides so the edges meet in the middle.

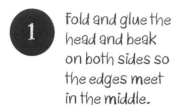

2 Fold the model in half.

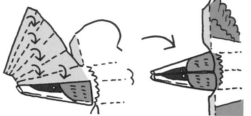

3 Fold the wing tabs over and glue them down on both sides.

4 Fold down the wings and fins.

5 Glue the back piece in place.

DONE!

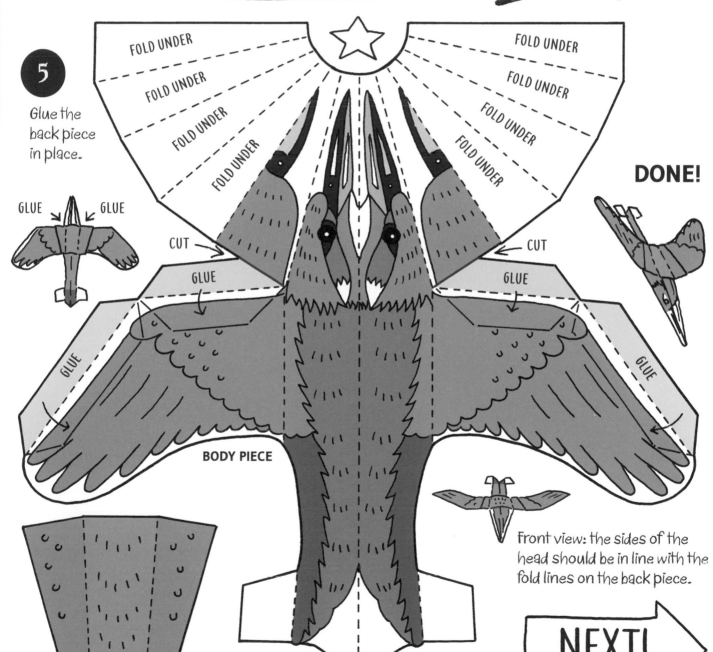

FOLD UNDER
FOLD UNDER
FOLD UNDER
FOLD UNDER

FOLD UNDER
FOLD UNDER
FOLD UNDER
FOLD UNDER

GLUE   GLUE

CUT

GLUE

GLUE

CUT

GLUE

GLUE

GLUE

BODY PIECE

BACK PIECE

Front view: the sides of the head should be in line with the fold lines on the back piece.

NEXT!

HOW TO FLY YOUR KINGFISHER

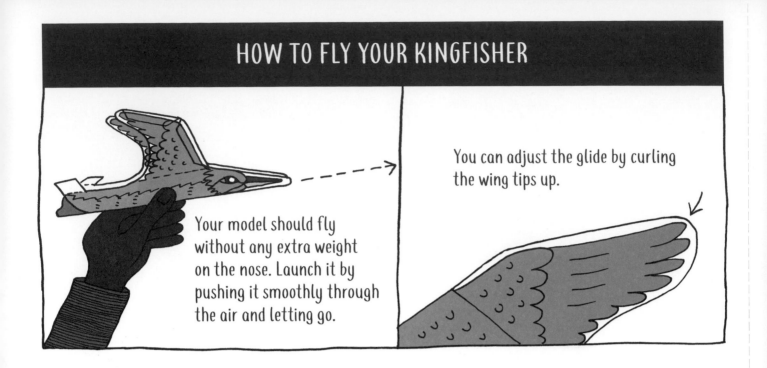

Your model should fly without any extra weight on the nose. Launch it by pushing it smoothly through the air and letting go.

You can adjust the glide by curling the wing tips up.

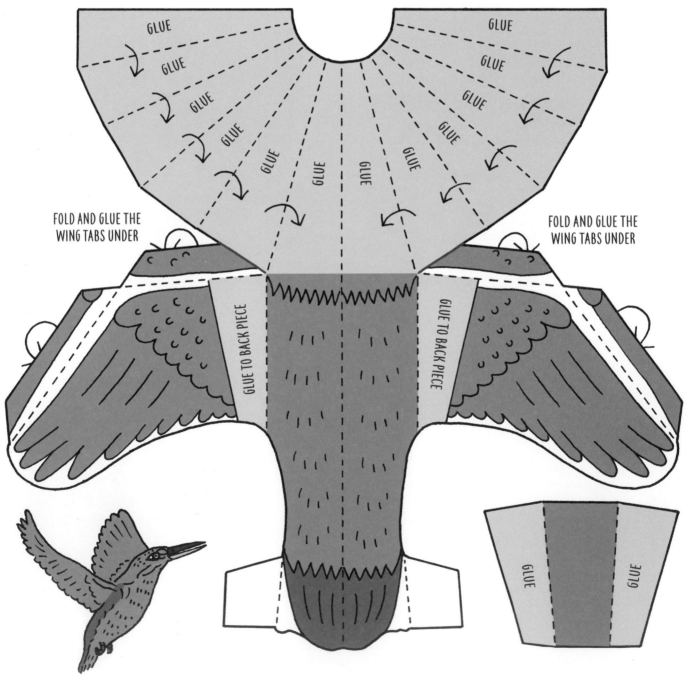

GLUE
GLUE
GLUE
GLUE
GLUE
GLUE
GLUE
GLUE
GLUE
GLUE
GLUE

FOLD AND GLUE THE WING TABS UNDER

FOLD AND GLUE THE WING TABS UNDER

GLUE TO BACK PIECE

GLUE TO BACK PIECE

GLUE

GLUE

COLUGO

Follow the steps to make this model:

- Cut along all the solid outlines
- Fold along the dotted lines
- Apply glue to all the green areas marked GLUE

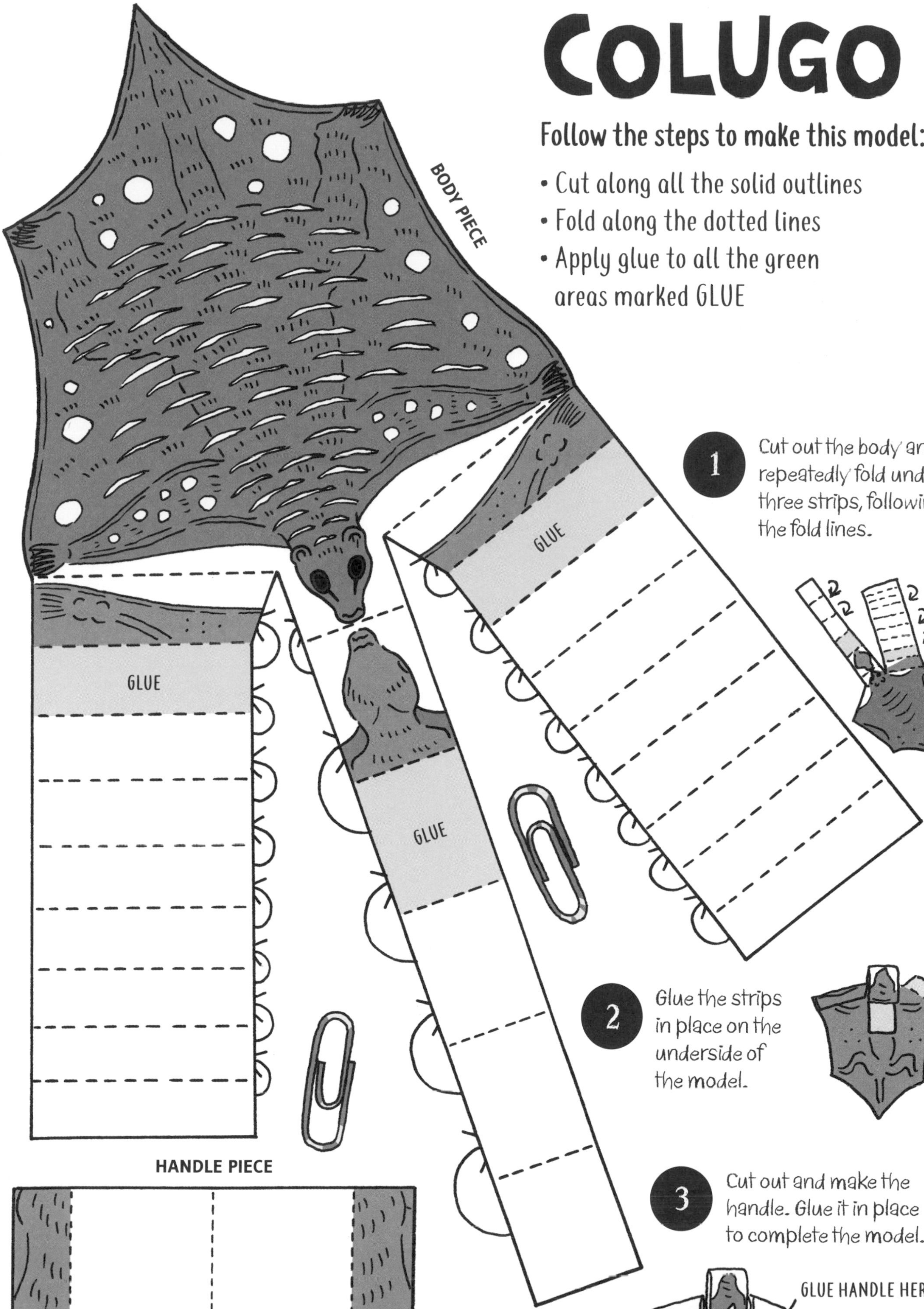

BODY PIECE

GLUE

GLUE

GLUE

1 Cut out the body and repeatedly fold under all three strips, following the fold lines.

2 Glue the strips in place on the underside of the model.

3 Cut out and make the handle. Glue it in place to complete the model.

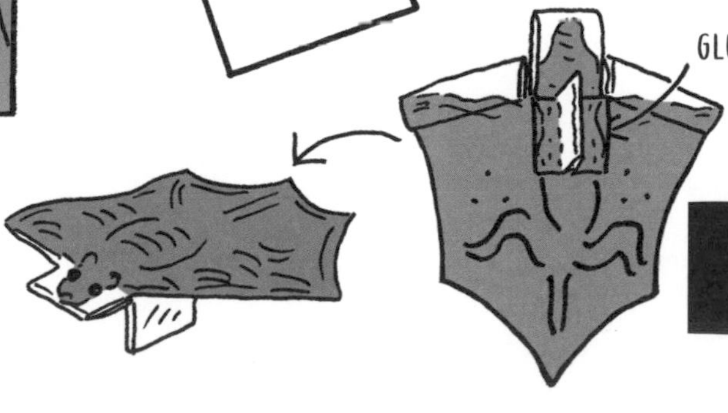

GLUE HANDLE HERE

HANDLE PIECE

FOLD UP

GLUE CLOSED

NEXT!

HOW TO FLY YOUR COLUGO

Your model should glide without any extra weight but you can make it more stable and help it to fly further by adding some paperclips to the head.

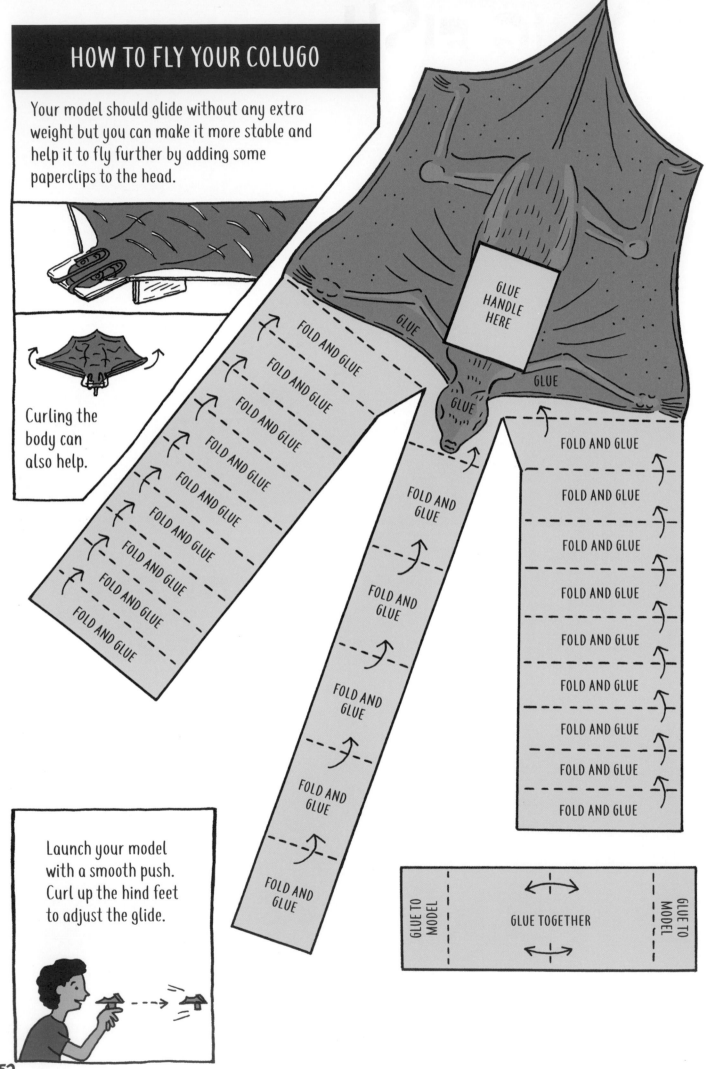

Curling the body can also help.

Launch your model with a smooth push. Curl up the hind feet to adjust the glide.

GLUE HANDLE HERE

GLUE

GLUE

GLUE

FOLD AND GLUE

FOLD AND GLUE

FOLD AND GLUE

FOLD AND GLUE

FOLD AND GLUE

FOLD AND GLUE

FOLD AND GLUE

FOLD AND GLUE

FOLD AND GLUE

FOLD AND GLUE

FOLD AND GLUE

FOLD AND GLUE

FOLD AND GLUE

FOLD AND GLUE

FOLD AND GLUE

FOLD AND GLUE

FOLD AND GLUE

FOLD AND GLUE

FOLD AND GLUE

FOLD AND GLUE

FOLD AND GLUE

FOLD AND GLUE

GLUE TO MODEL

GLUE TOGETHER

GLUE TO MODEL

FLYING FISH

Follow the steps to make this model:

- Cut along all the solid outlines
- Fold along the dotted lines
- Apply glue to all the green areas marked GLUE

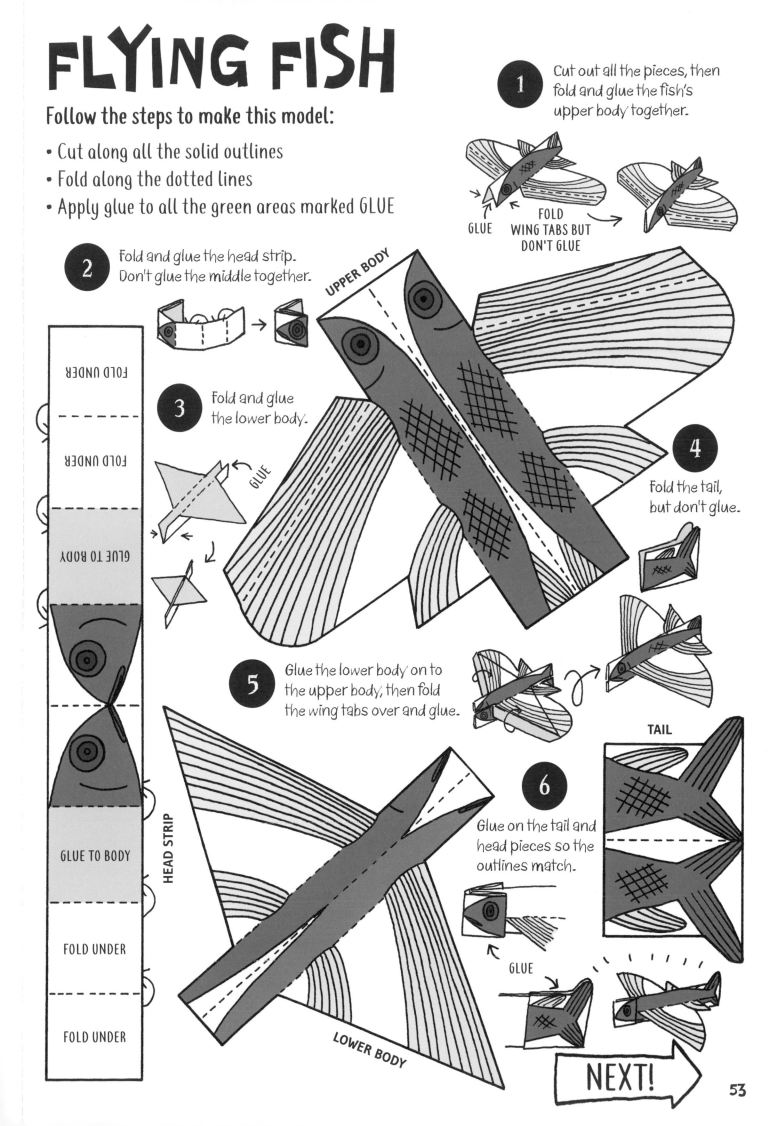

1 Cut out all the pieces, then fold and glue the fish's upper body together.

GLUE

FOLD WING TABS BUT DON'T GLUE

2 Fold and glue the head strip. Don't glue the middle together.

3 Fold and glue the lower body.

GLUE

4 Fold the tail, but don't glue.

5 Glue the lower body on to the upper body, then fold the wing tabs over and glue.

6 Glue on the tail and head pieces so the outlines match.

GLUE

UPPER BODY

TAIL

HEAD STRIP

LOWER BODY

FOLD UNDER

FOLD UNDER

GLUE TO BODY

GLUE TO BODY

FOLD UNDER

FOLD UNDER

NEXT!

HOW TO FLY YOUR FLYING FISH

Add one or more paperclips to the head.

Gently curl up the tips of the front and rear fins.

Launch with a pushing motion and adjust the fins as needed.

WING TAB

GLUE TO UNDERSIDE

GLUE TOGETHER

GLUE TOGETHER

CURL FINS

GLUE TO UNDERSIDE

WING TAB

GLUE

GLUE

GLUE

GLUE

GLUE

GLUE

GLUE

GLUE

GLUE

GLUE

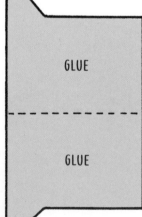

GLUE

GLUE

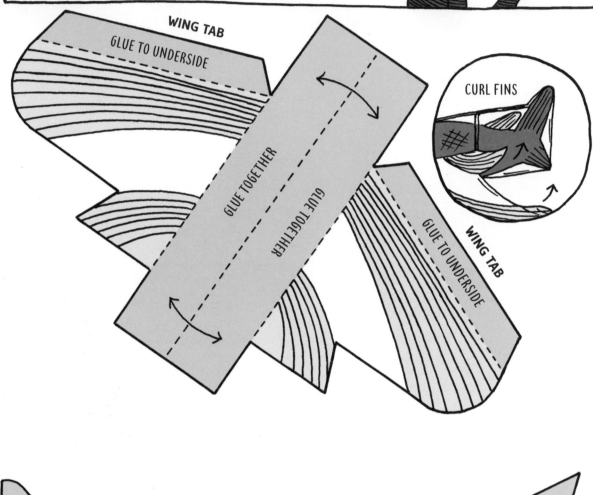

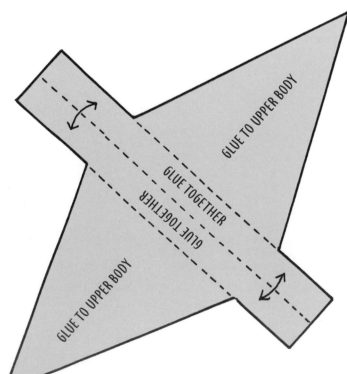

GLUE TO UPPER BODY

GLUE TOGETHER

GLUE TOGETHER

GLUE TO UPPER BODY

FLYING SEEDS

Follow the steps to make these models:
- Cut along all the solid outlines
- Fold along the dotted lines
- Apply glue to all the green areas marked GLUE

1 Cut out the pieces for the whirling nut seed. Fold the vanes over along the fold lines and glue in place.

2 Fold the vane piece in half and glue it closed.

3 Glue the vanes on to the seed piece and fold the seed piece around in number order.

4 Glue the seed piece closed.

5 Spread the vanes out.

6 Add paperclips.

1 Cut out the Javan cucumber seed. Fold up the strip and glue it to the seed.

It's ready to fly!

JAVAN CUCUMBER SEED

WHIRLING NUT SEED (SEED PIECE)

GLUE

CUT HERE

WHIRLING NUT SEED (VANES)

CUT HERE

IT'S DONE!

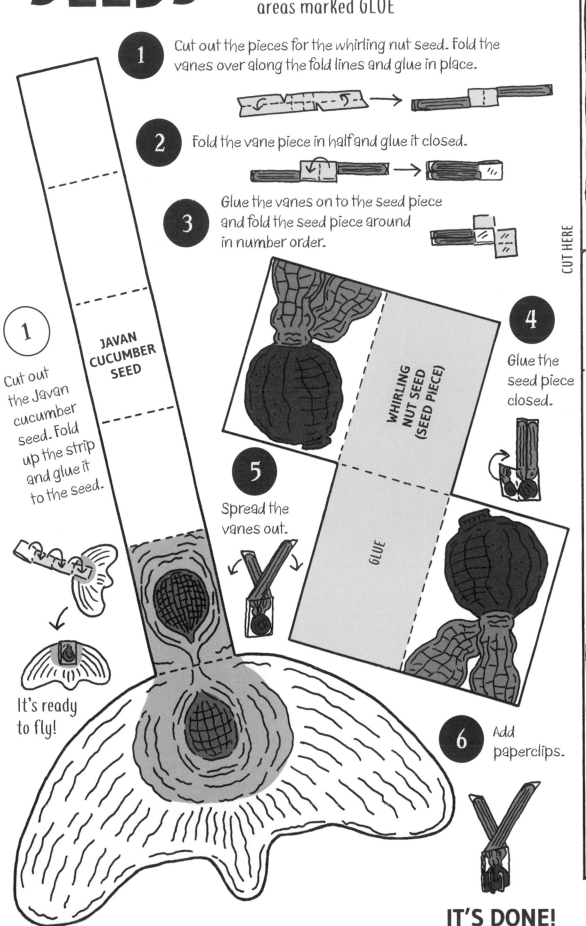

55

HOW TO FLY YOUR SEEDS

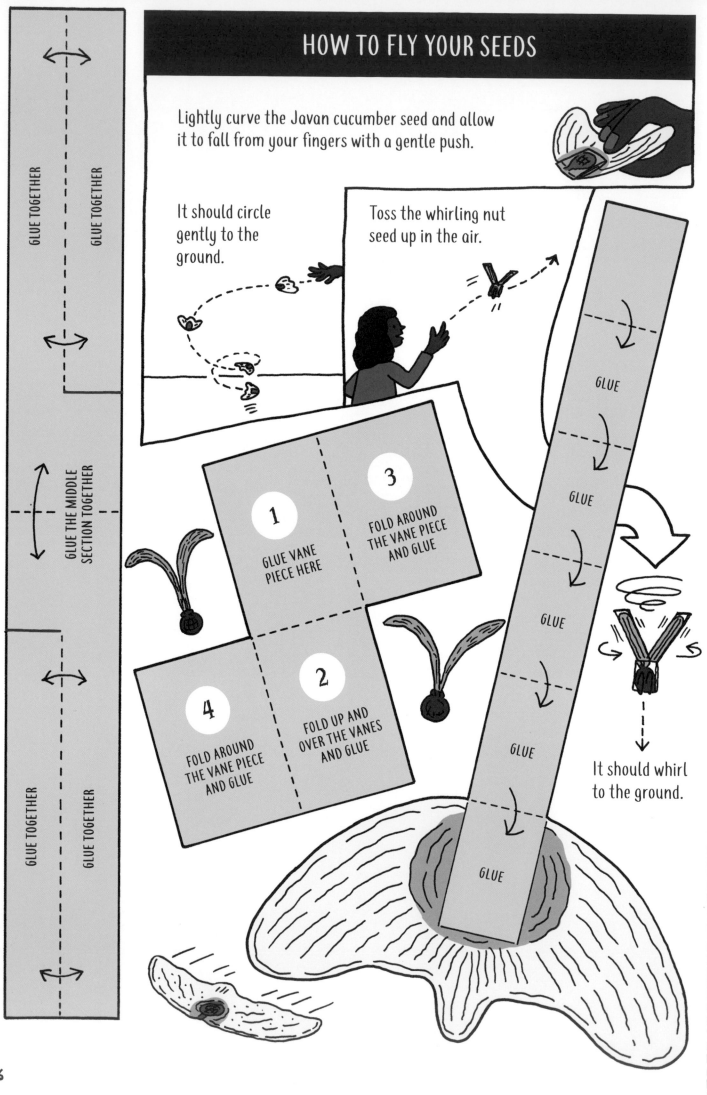

Lightly curve the Javan cucumber seed and allow it to fall from your fingers with a gentle push.

It should circle gently to the ground.

Toss the whirling nut seed up in the air.

It should whirl to the ground.

1 GLUE VANE PIECE HERE

3 FOLD AROUND THE VANE PIECE AND GLUE

4 FOLD AROUND THE VANE PIECE AND GLUE

2 FOLD UP AND OVER THE VANES AND GLUE

GLUE TOGETHER

GLUE TOGETHER

GLUE THE MIDDLE SECTION TOGETHER

GLUE TOGETHER

GLUE TOGETHER

GLUE

GLUE

GLUE

GLUE

GLUE

GLUE

BOOMERANG

Follow the steps to make this model:

- Cut along all the solid outlines
- Fold along the dotted lines
- Apply glue to all the green areas marked GLUE

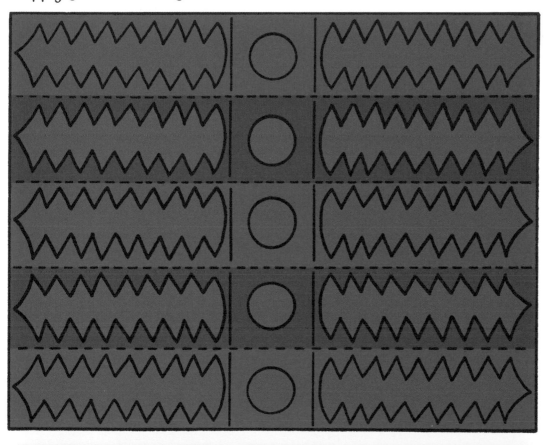

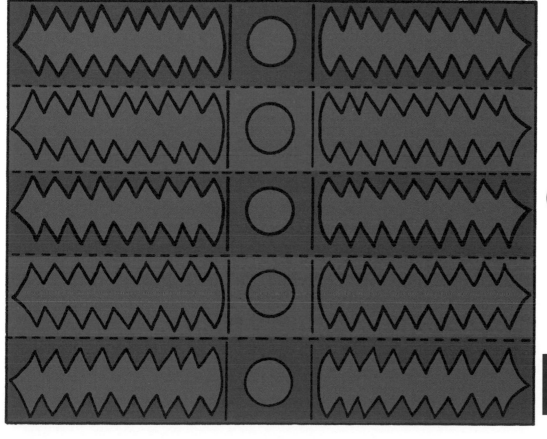

1 Fold along the dashed lines to make two arms.

2 Glue each arm shut.

3 Glue both arms together at the centre, or join them using a tight rubber band.

OR

4 Gently curve the end of each arm.

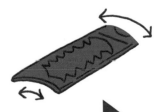

HOW TO FLY YOUR BOOMERANG

Launch it upwards into the air at an angle, sending it spinning.

With practice, it should rise, turn and head back to you.

Fly your boomerang in a large, open area.

Throw your boomerang upwards at an angle of about 30°.

It should fly up, turn and come back.

Can you catch it in your hand?

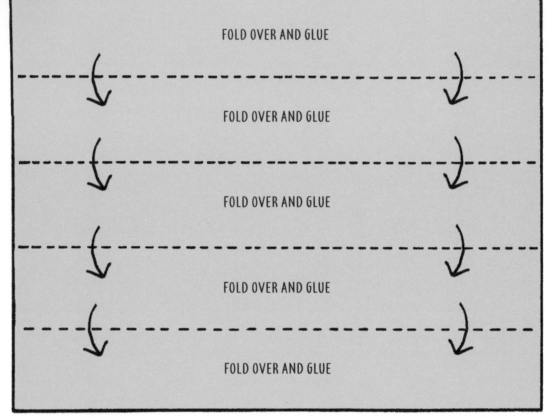

FOLD OVER AND GLUE

FOLD OVER AND GLUE

FOLD OVER AND GLUE

FOLD OVER AND GLUE

FOLD OVER AND GLUE

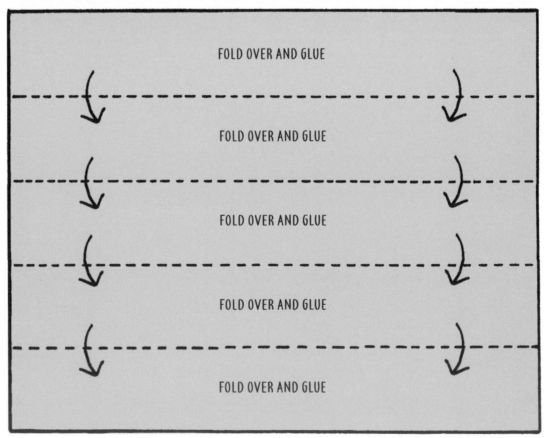

FOLD OVER AND GLUE

FOLD OVER AND GLUE

FOLD OVER AND GLUE

FOLD OVER AND GLUE

FOLD OVER AND GLUE

DRAGON DART

Follow the steps to make this model:

- Cut along all the solid outlines
- Fold along the dotted lines

 1 Cut out the sheet and turn it over.

 2 Fold the sheet in half.

 3 Crease firmly and then unfold.

 **4** Fold each of the top corners to the middle crease.

 **5** Fold the top edges to the middle crease again on both sides.

 **6** Fold the tip down, as shown.

 NEXT!

59

HOW TO FLY YOUR DRAGON DART

Launch your plane with a pushing motion — like throwing a dart.

If your model dips in front, gently curl up the wing tips.

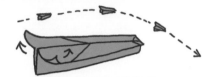

If your model rises and stalls, curl the wings down.

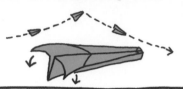

7

Fold your model in half.

8

Fold the edges of the wings to the middle crease.

9

Fold up the wings.

DONE!

KITE

Follow the steps to make this model:

- Cut along all the solid outlines
- Fold along the dotted lines
- Apply glue to all the green areas marked GLUE

风筝

风筝

1

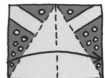

Start with the back of the kite facing up and fold in half.

2

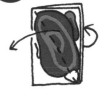

Fold down the sides along the fold lines.

3

Glue the middle together.

4

Open out the kite.

STRUT

NEXT

5 Follow these instructions to make the strut.

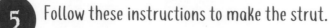

Fold it in half.

Fold up the edges of both sides.

Glue the middle closed.

Flip it over.

6

Glue the strut in place on the kite.

7

Ask an adult to pierce a hole through the white dots and strengthen it with tape.

8

Add string or thread.

DONE!

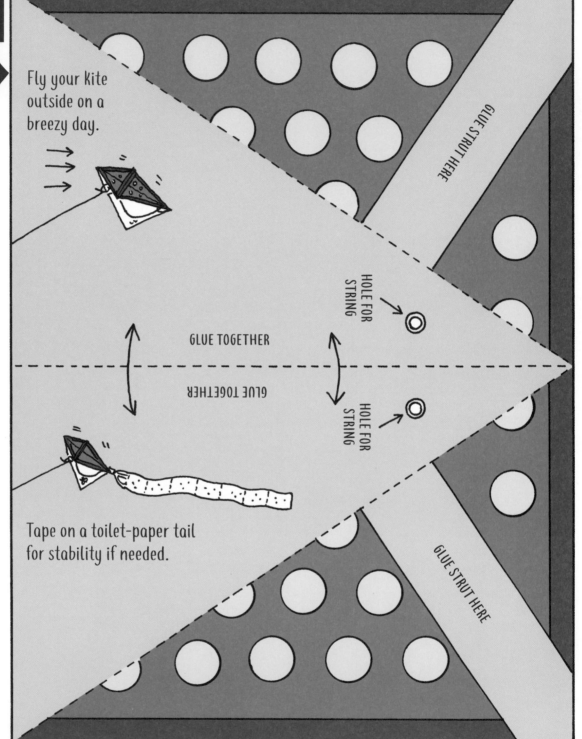

Fly your kite outside on a breezy day.

GLUE STRUT HERE

HOLE FOR STRING

GLUE TOGETHER

GLUE TOGETHER

HOLE FOR STRING

GLUE STRUT HERE

Tape on a toilet-paper tail for stability if needed.

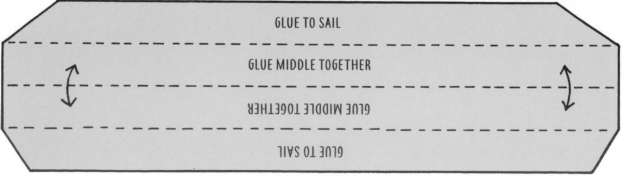

GLUE TO SAIL

GLUE MIDDLE TOGETHER

GLUE MIDDLE TOGETHER

GLUE TO SAIL

CLEM SOHN

Follow the steps to make this model:

- Cut along all the solid lines
- Fold along the dotted lines
- Apply glue to all the green areas marked GLUE

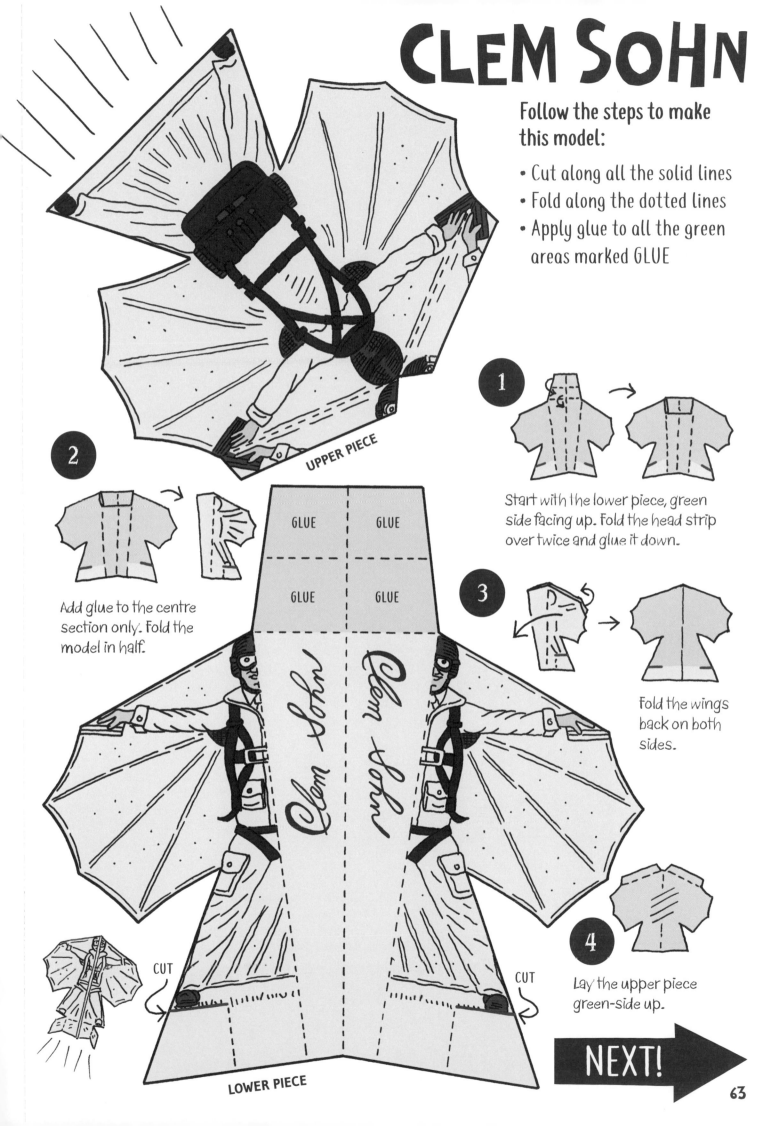

UPPER PIECE

1

Start with the lower piece, green side facing up. Fold the head strip over twice and glue it down.

2

Add glue to the centre section only. Fold the model in half.

3

Fold the wings back on both sides.

GLUE   GLUE

GLUE   GLUE

Clem Sohn

Clem Sohn

4

Lay the upper piece green-side up.

CUT

CUT

LOWER PIECE

NEXT!

5

Glue the lower and upper pieces together, leaving the wing tabs sticking out.

GLUE

6

Fold the wing tabs over and glue them in place on the lower piece.

HOW TO FLY YOUR GLIDER

The model will glide nicely indoors, but try throwing it outside too, launching it upwards fairly hard.

With practice, the model can do loops and rolls before gliding.

WING TAB

GLUE

GLUE TO LOWER PIECE

GLUE TO LOWER PIECE

GLUE

WING TAB

7 Curl up the wing tips. Fold down the rear stabilizers.

FRONT VIEW

GLUE   GLUE

GLUE HERE   GLUE HERE

GLUE TO UPPER PIECE   GLUE TO UPPER PIECE

8

Add paperclips to finish.

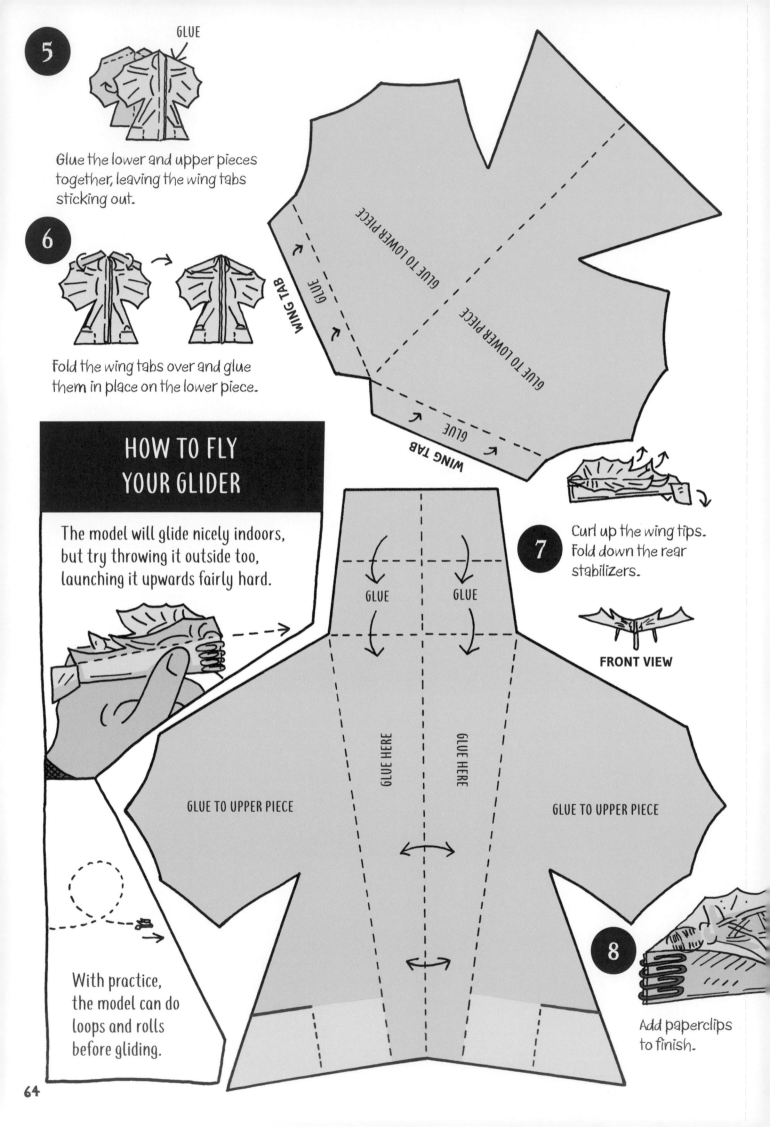

64

CAYLEY GLIDER

Follow the steps to make this model:

- Cut along all the solid outlines
- Fold along the dotted lines
- Apply glue to all the green areas marked GLUE

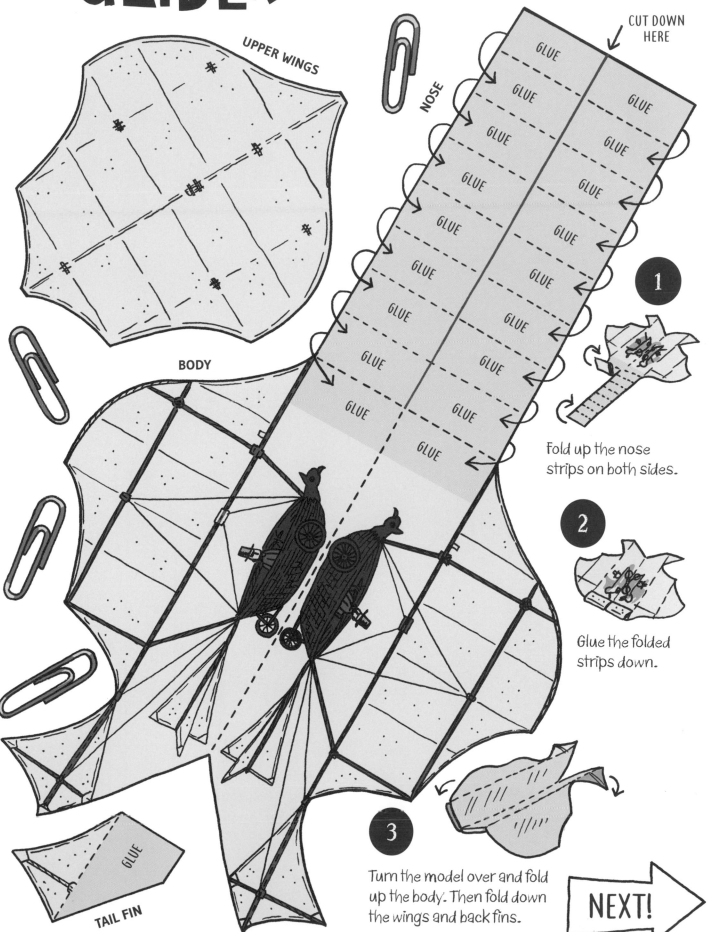

UPPER WINGS

NOSE

CUT DOWN HERE

GLUE

BODY

TAIL FIN

GLUE

1 Fold up the nose strips on both sides.

2 Glue the folded strips down.

3 Turn the model over and fold up the body. Then fold down the wings and back fins.

NEXT!

HOW TO FLY YOUR GLIDER

Add three or four paperclips to the nose for balance.
Launch your glider with a gentle push.

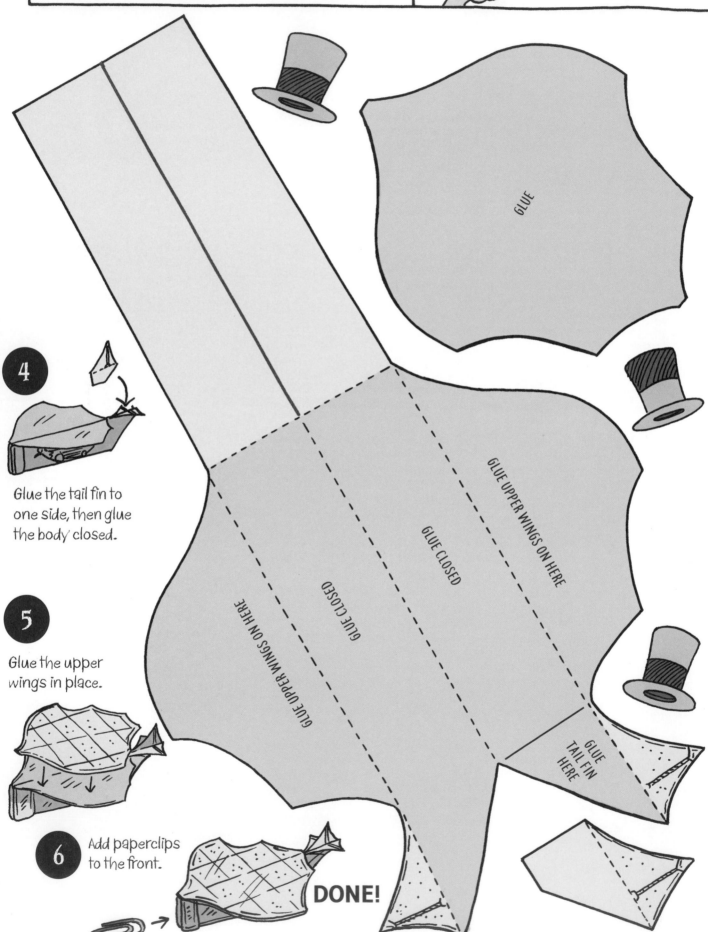

4

Glue the tail fin to one side, then glue the body closed.

5

Glue the upper wings in place.

GLUE

GLUE UPPER WINGS ON HERE

GLUE CLOSED

GLUE CLOSED

GLUE UPPER WINGS ON HERE

GLUE TAIL FIN HERE

6 Add paperclips to the front.

DONE!

LILIENTHAL GLIDER

Follow the steps to make this model:

- Cut along all the solid outlines
- Fold along the dotted lines
- Apply glue to all the green areas marked GLUE

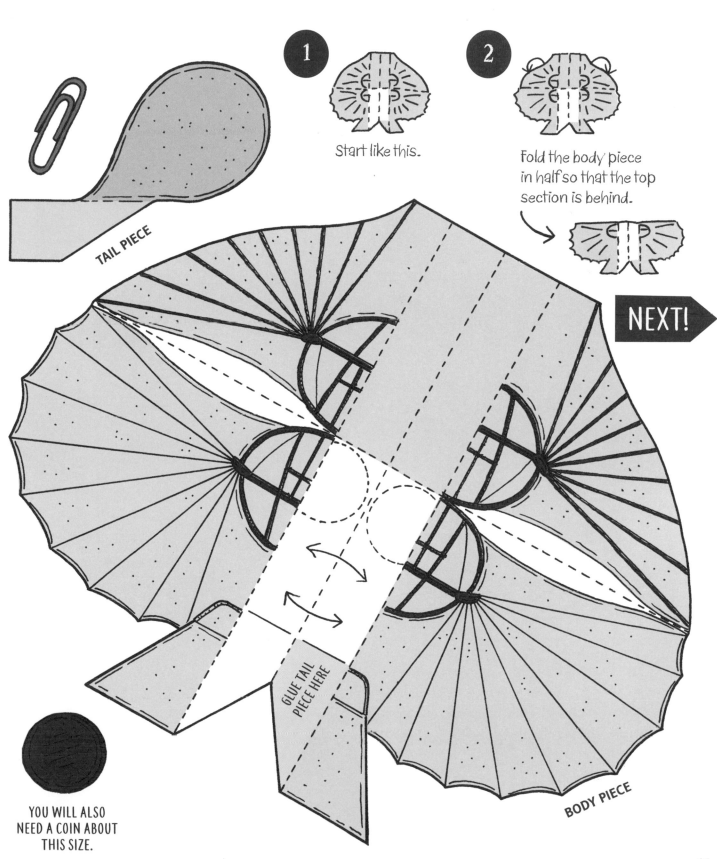

TAIL PIECE

1 Start like this.

2 Fold the body piece in half so that the top section is behind.

NEXT!

GLUE TAIL PIECE HERE

BODY PIECE

YOU WILL ALSO NEED A COIN ABOUT THIS SIZE.

3 Glue the tail piece in place inside the body.

4 Fold the body in half.

5 Fold the wings down.

6 Insert a small coin into the nose space.

7 Secure with paperclips.

DONE!

HOW TO FLY YOUR GLIDER

Launch your model with a gentle push. The coin makes the glider heavy, so be careful where you aim it.

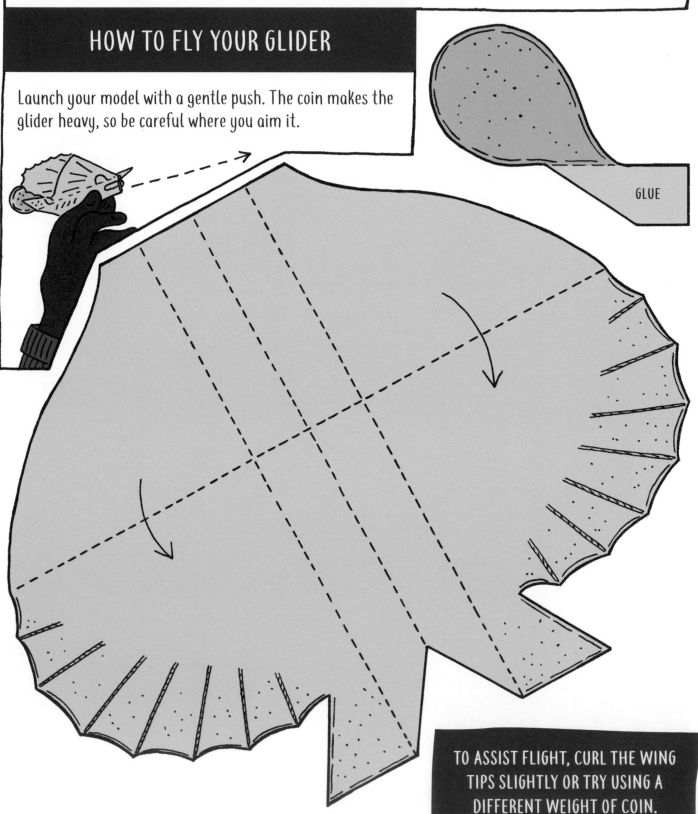

GLUE

TO ASSIST FLIGHT, CURL THE WING TIPS SLIGHTLY OR TRY USING A DIFFERENT WEIGHT OF COIN.

WRIGHT FLYER 1

Follow the steps to make this model:

- Cut along all the solid outlines
- Fold along the dotted lines
- Apply glue to all the green areas marked GLUE

1 Fold the main wing piece over and glue together.

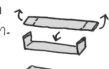

2 Fold the sides up. The side with the letter on should be underneath.

3 Fold and glue the top wing piece in place.

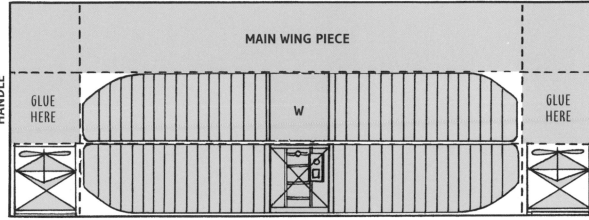

HANDLE

GLUE GLUE GLUE GLUE

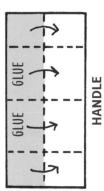

MAIN WING PIECE

GLUE HERE

W

GLUE HERE

TOP WING PIECE

4 Repeat steps 1–3 to make the elevator.

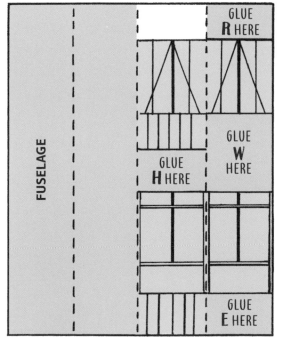

FUSELAGE

GLUE **R** HERE

GLUE **W** HERE

GLUE **H** HERE

GLUE **E** HERE

5 Fold the handle in half lengthways and glue. Then fold along the three fold lines and glue as below.

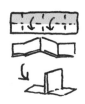

E

MAIN ELEVATOR PIECE

TOP ELEVATOR PIECE

RUDDER

6 Fold the fuselage.

7 Glue closed.

8 Fold and glue the rudder.

N E X T

HOW TO FLY YOUR MODEL

Launch your model using the handle. It should glide smoothly.

Adjust the flight by tweaking the wings and elevator.

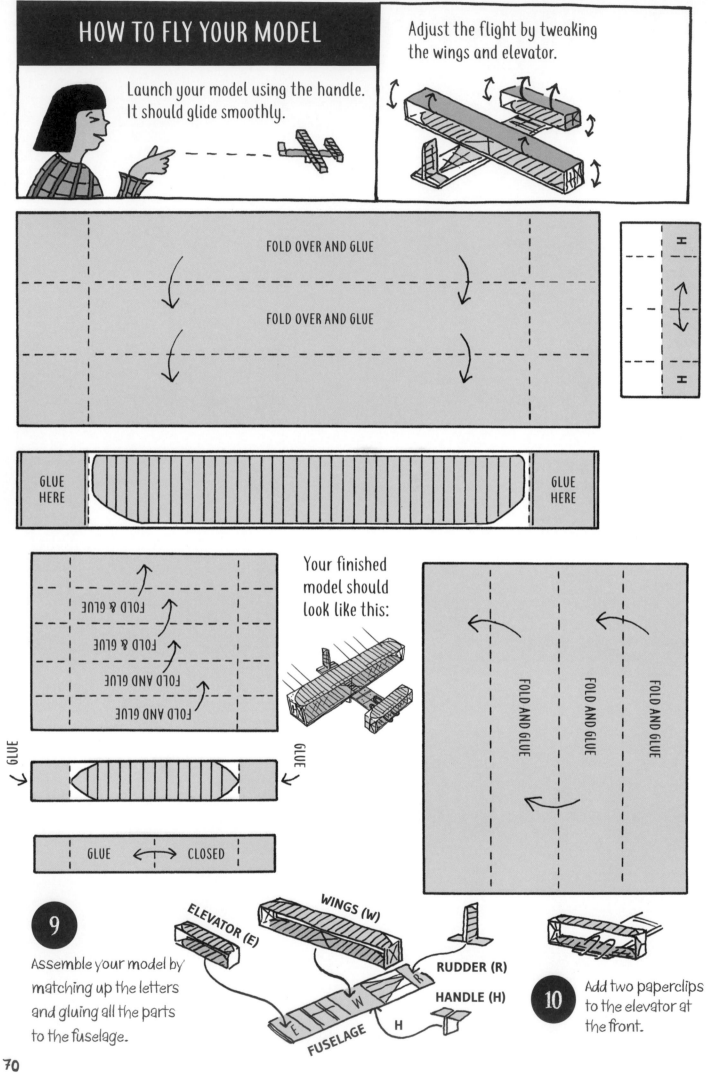

FOLD OVER AND GLUE

FOLD OVER AND GLUE

H

H

GLUE
HERE

GLUE
HERE

FOLD & GLUE

FOLD & GLUE

FOLD AND GLUE

FOLD AND GLUE

GLUE

GLUE

Your finished
model should
look like this:

FOLD AND GLUE

FOLD AND GLUE

FOLD AND GLUE

GLUE ⟷ CLOSED

9 Assemble your model by matching up the letters and gluing all the parts to the fuselage.

ELEVATOR (E)

WINGS (W)

RUDDER (R)

HANDLE (H)

FUSELAGE

10 Add two paperclips to the elevator at the front.

BLÉRIOT XI MONOPLANE

Follow the steps to make this model:

- Cut along all the solid outlines
- Fold along the dotted lines
- Apply glue to all the green areas marked GLUE

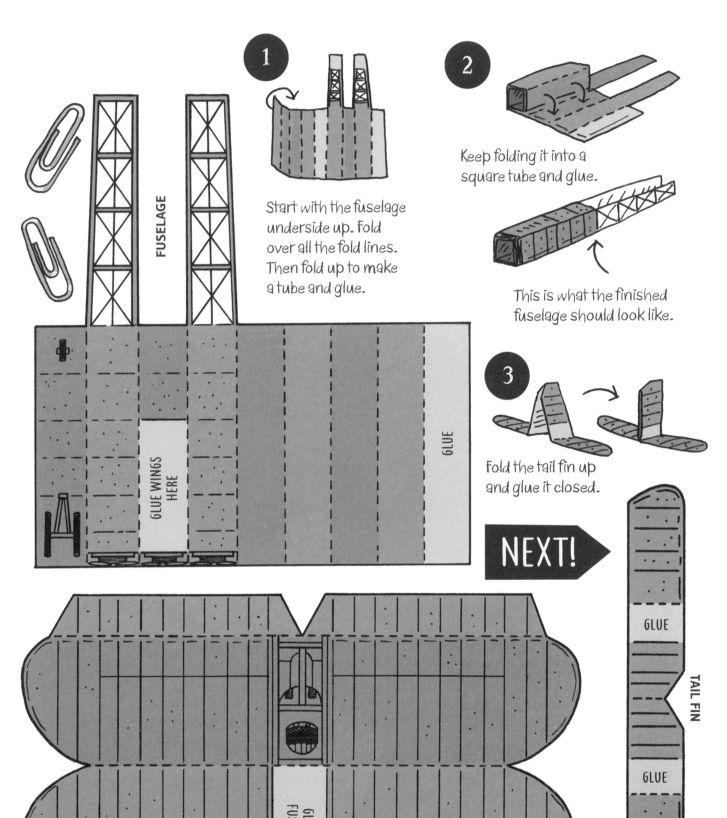

FUSELAGE

1 Start with the fuselage underside up. Fold over all the fold lines. Then fold up to make a tube and glue.

2 Keep folding it into a square tube and glue.

This is what the finished fuselage should look like.

3 Fold the tail fin up and glue it closed.

NEXT!

GLUE WINGS HERE

GLUE

GLUE TO FUSELAGE

WING PIECE

TAIL FIN

GLUE

GLUE

4 Start with the wing piece green-side up. Fold in half and glue it closed.

5 Fold the wing tabs over and glue them down.

6 Glue the tail fin inside the ends of the fuselage. It should point up, as shown.

GLUE   GLUE

7 Glue the wings on to the fuselage.

8 Add four paperclips to the nose to finish it.

HOW TO FLY YOUR MODEL

Launch your model with a gentle push. Adjust the wings and tail fin for the best glide.

Watch it fly!

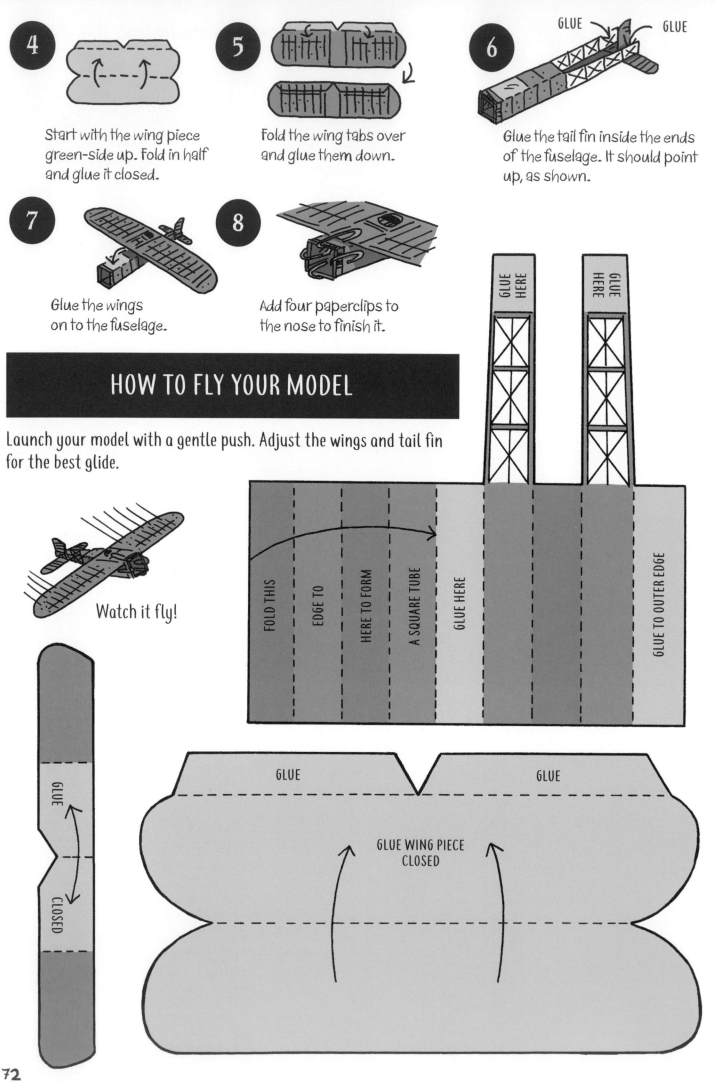

GLUE HERE

GLUE HERE

FOLD THIS EDGE TO HERE TO FORM A SQUARE TUBE GLUE HERE

GLUE TO OUTER EDGE

GLUE

CLOSED

GLUE

GLUE

GLUE WING PIECE CLOSED

HELICOPTER BLADES

Follow the steps to make this model:

- Cut along all the solid outlines
- Fold along the dotted lines
- Apply glue to all the green areas marked GLUE

1 Begin green-side up.

2 Repeatedly fold the edge over on the fold lines and glue down.

3 Fold the strip lengthways and glue it down.

4 Wind the strip tightly around the bottom of the blade.

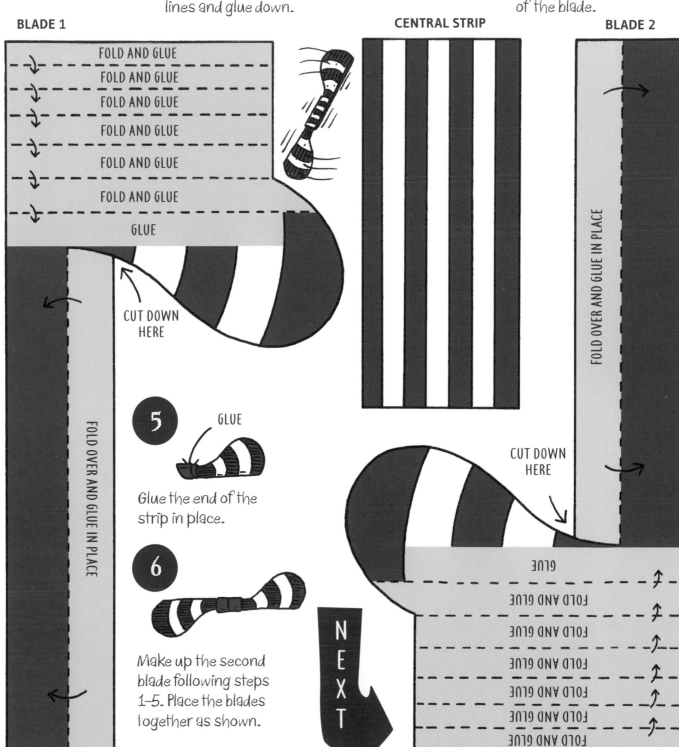

BLADE 1

FOLD AND GLUE
FOLD AND GLUE
FOLD AND GLUE
FOLD AND GLUE
FOLD AND GLUE
FOLD AND GLUE
GLUE

CUT DOWN HERE

FOLD OVER AND GLUE IN PLACE

CENTRAL STRIP

BLADE 2

FOLD OVER AND GLUE IN PLACE

CUT DOWN HERE

GLUE
FOLD AND GLUE
FOLD AND GLUE
FOLD AND GLUE
FOLD AND GLUE
FOLD AND GLUE
FOLD AND GLUE

5 GLUE

Glue the end of the strip in place.

6 Make up the second blade following steps 1–5. Place the blades together as shown.

NEXT

73

HOW TO LAUNCH YOUR HELICOPTER BLADES

Gently curl down the curved edge of each blade.

Toss the model high into the air.

It should spin and look like rings of colour as it falls.

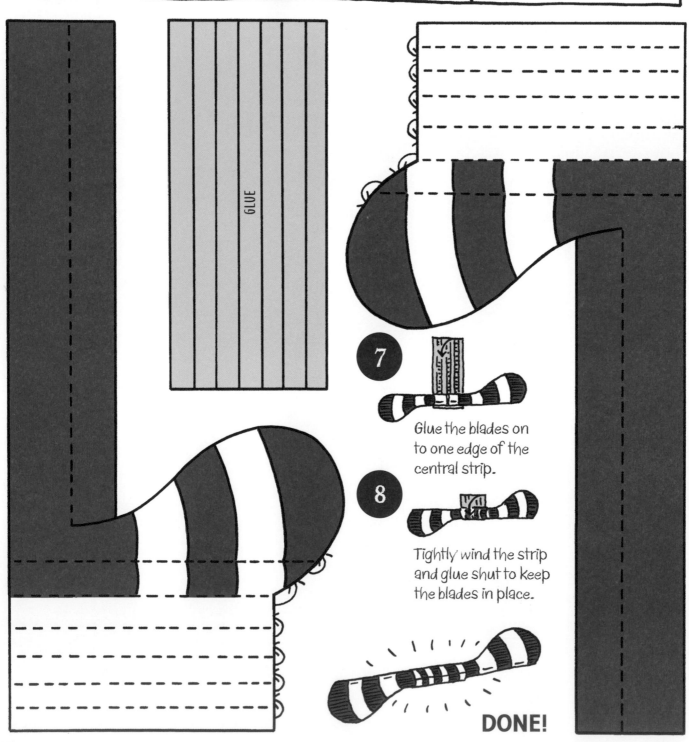

GLUE

7 Glue the blades on to one edge of the central strip.

8 Tightly wind the strip and glue shut to keep the blades in place.

DONE!

HANG-GLIDER

Follow the steps to make this model:

- Cut along all the solid outlines
- Fold along the dotted lines
- Apply glue to all the green areas marked GLUE

1 Start with the underside facing up. Fold over the left side along the crease line and glue tab 1 in place.

The wings should bow slightly.

WING PIECE

GLUE PILOT HERE

GLUE PILOT HERE

GLUE TAB 2

2 Fold the right side down along the fold line and glue tab 2 in place.

BOTH WINGS SHOULD BOW EQUALLY

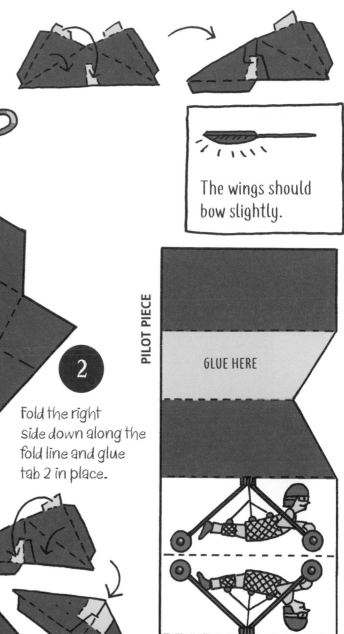

PILOT PIECE

GLUE HERE

GLUE HERE

CONTINUED ON NEXT PAGE ...

3 Make up the pilot piece as shown here:

With the pilot facing down, fold the edges to the middle.

Fold in half.

Fold down the top sections on both sides.

Finished pilot piece.

4

Glue the pilot in place on the underside of the wing.

5 Add four or more paperclips to the front of the pilot piece.

CURL UP WING FLAPS

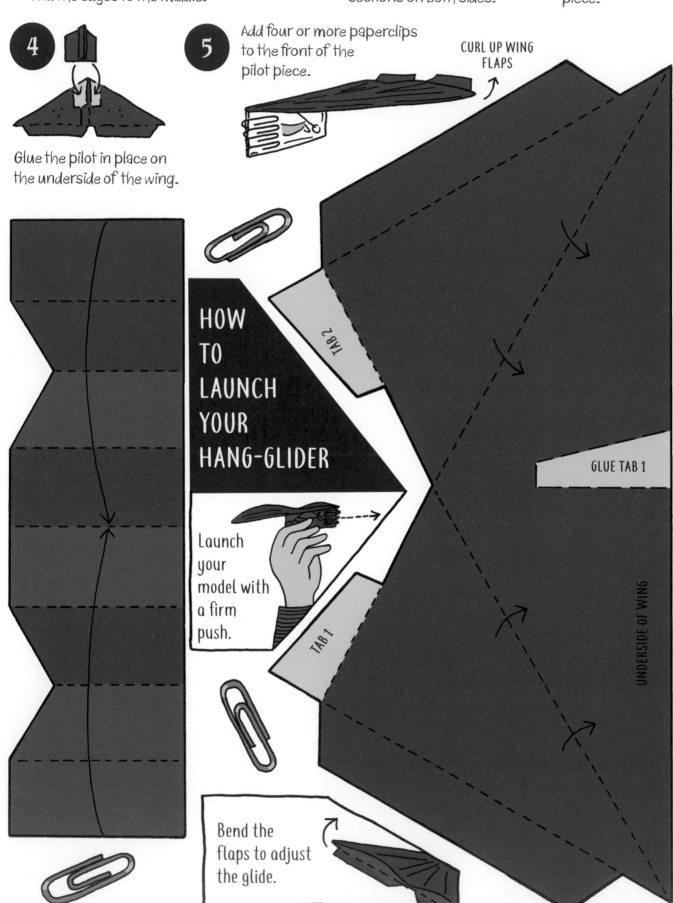

HOW TO LAUNCH YOUR HANG-GLIDER

Launch your model with a firm push.

TAB 2

GLUE TAB 1

TAB 1

UNDERSIDE OF WING

Bend the flaps to adjust the glide.

CONCORDE

Follow the steps to make this model:

- Cut along all the solid outlines
- Fold along the dotted lines
- Apply glue to all the green areas marked GLUE

TAIL FIN

BODY

MAKE SHARP CREASES

1 Fold the top corners to the middle and crease.

2 Fold the top edges to the middle and crease.

3 Fold the edges to the middle again and crease.

GLUE TAIL FIN HERE

MAKE A SHORT SNIP TO FREE THE ELEVATOR

MAKE A SHORT SNIP TO FREE THE ELEVATOR

NEXT!

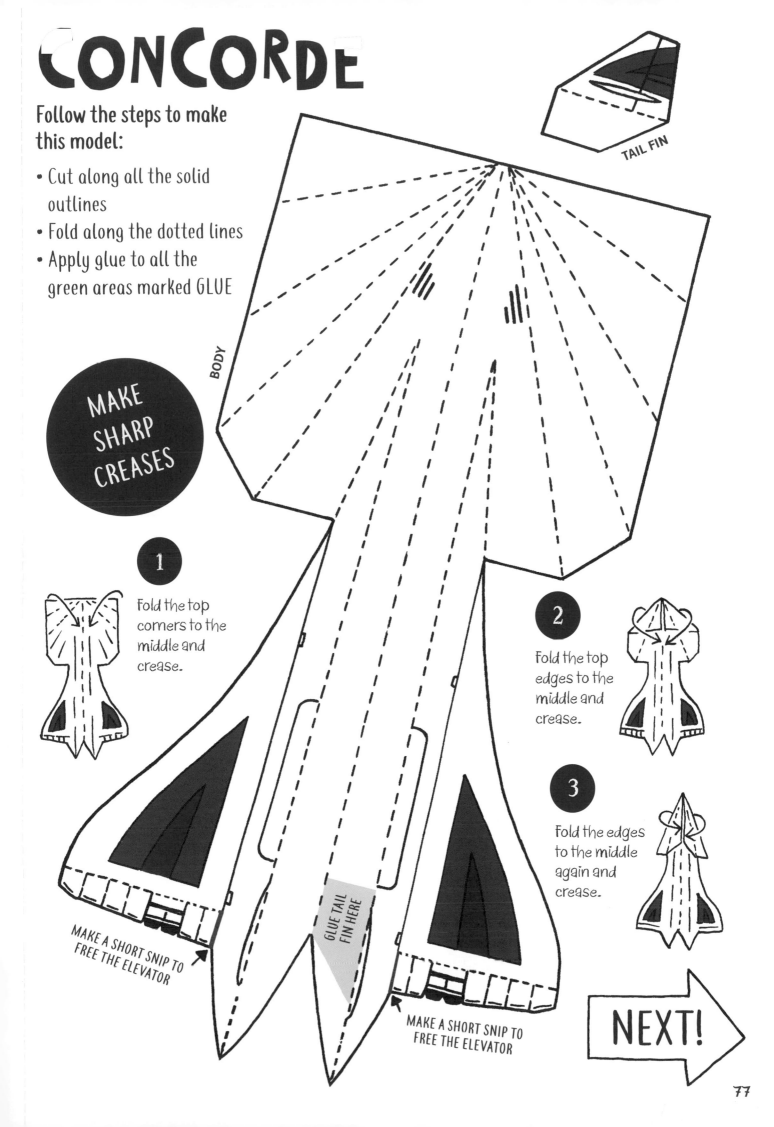

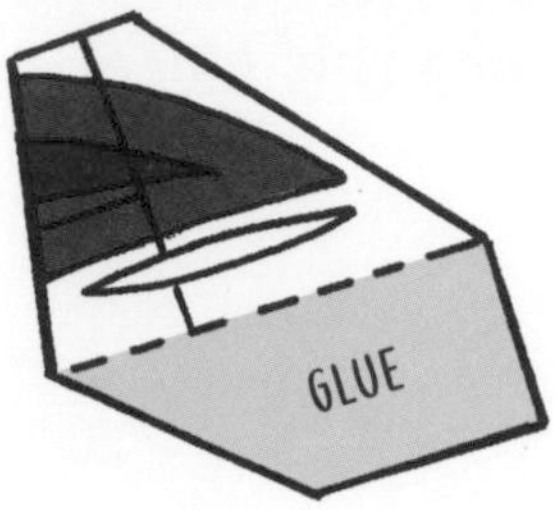

GLUE

Launch your model as though you are throwing
a dart. It can fly well over 10 metres!

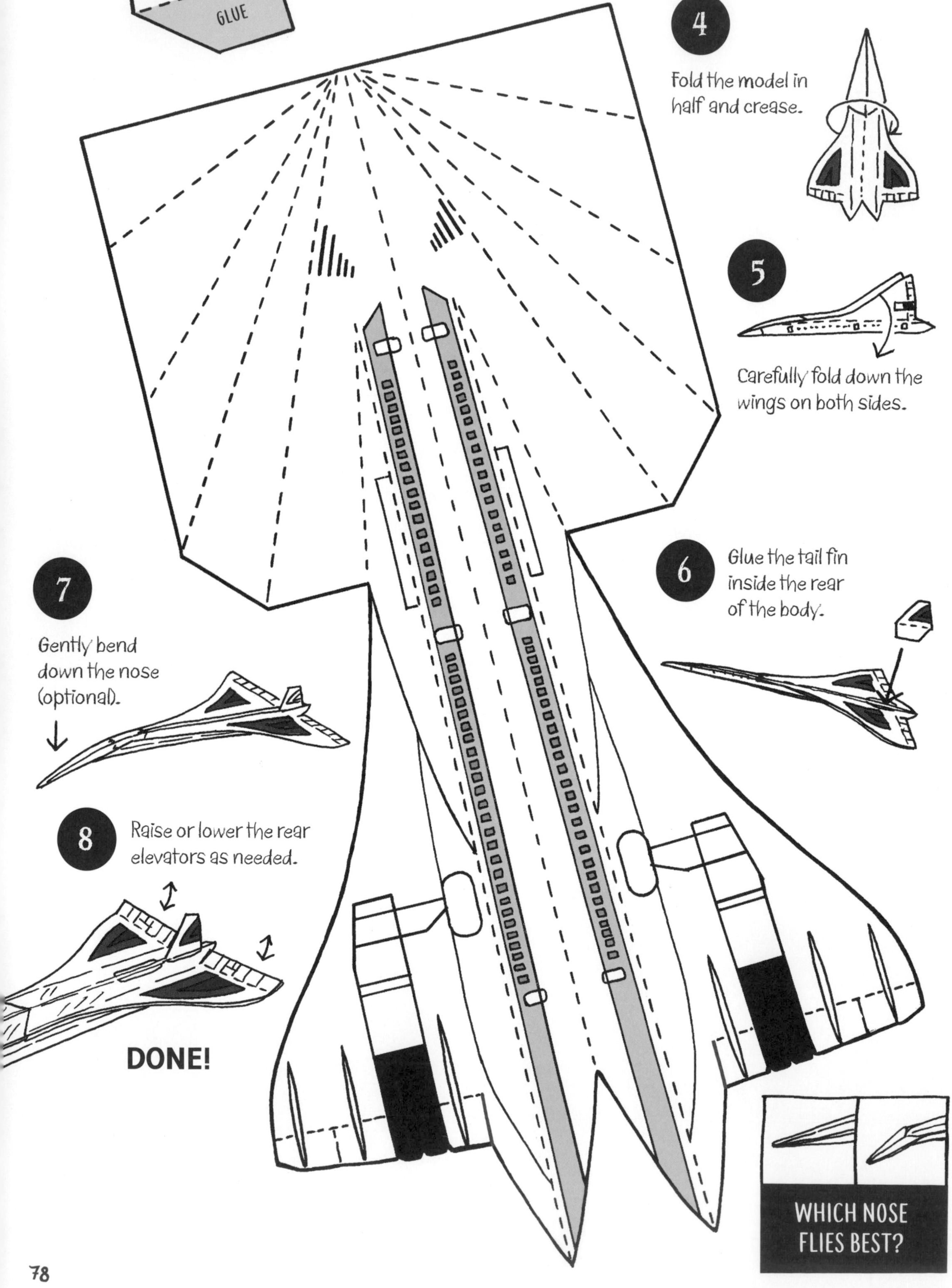

4

Fold the model in
half and crease.

5

Carefully fold down the
wings on both sides.

6

Glue the tail fin
inside the rear
of the body.

7

Gently bend
down the nose
(optional).

8

Raise or lower the rear
elevators as needed.

DONE!

WHICH NOSE
FLIES BEST?

SPACE SHUTTLE

Follow the steps to make this model:

- Cut along all the solid outlines
- Fold along the dotted lines
- Apply glue to all the green areas marked GLUE

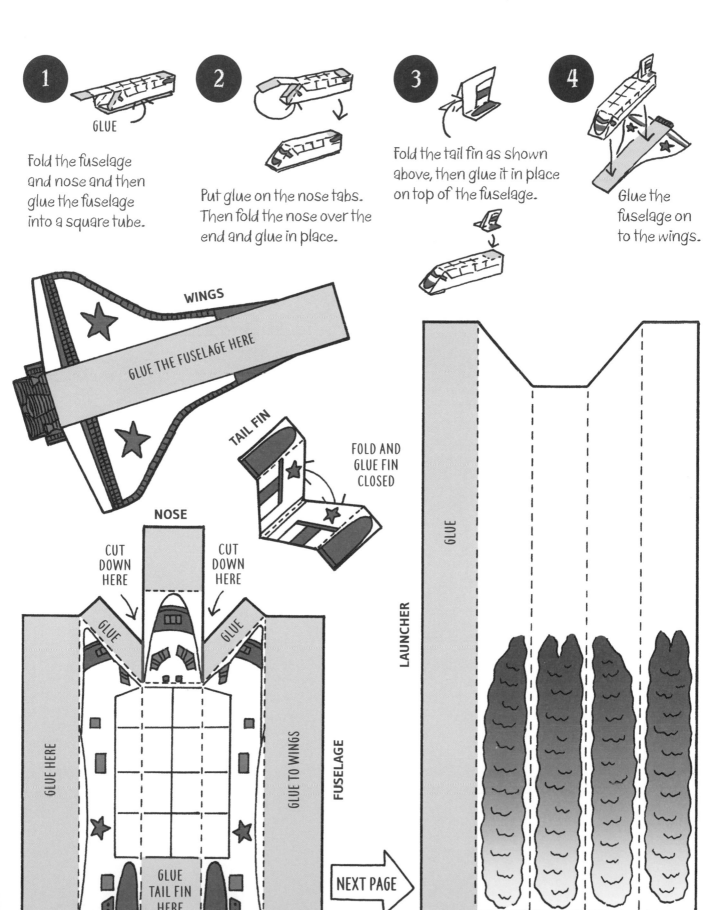

1 GLUE

Fold the fuselage and nose and then glue the fuselage into a square tube.

2 Put glue on the nose tabs. Then fold the nose over the end and glue in place.

3 Fold the tail fin as shown above, then glue it in place on top of the fuselage.

4 Glue the fuselage on to the wings.

WINGS

GLUE THE FUSELAGE HERE

TAIL FIN

FOLD AND GLUE FIN CLOSED

NOSE

CUT DOWN HERE

CUT DOWN HERE

GLUE

GLUE

GLUE HERE

GLUE TO WINGS

FUSELAGE

GLUE TAIL FIN HERE

GLUE

LAUNCHER

NEXT PAGE

5

Fold and glue the launcher into a square tube.

6

Waterproof the end of the launcher with sticky tape.

7

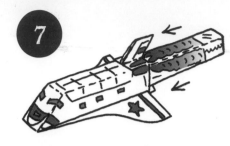

Insert the launcher firmly inside the fuselage. Your shuttle is ready for take-off.

HOW TO LAUNCH YOUR SPACE SHUTTLE

Blow sharply into the launcher tube. Adjust the wings if needed.

You can also try firing your model straight up into the air.

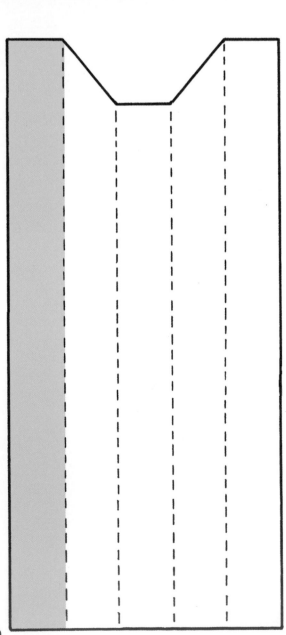

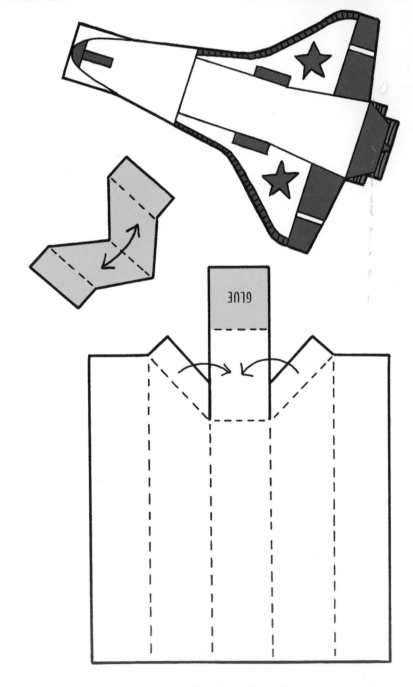

GLUE